D0458561

Praise for *Unshakable Hope*

"I firmly believe God has anointed my dear friend Max Lucado with a gift to communicate His heart to this generation. In his fortieth book, he shares how God's promises give us a firm foundation on which we can build our lives. The truth is, once you believe the promises of God, you not only have hope, your life is forever changed!"

—ROBERT MORRIS, FOUNDING SENIOR PASTOR, GATEWAY CHURCH; BESTSELLING AUTHOR OF *THE BLESSED LIFE*, *THE GOD I NEVER KNEW*, AND *FREQUENCY*

"Where do we find our hope and strength when the realities of life devastate and depress us? I love how Max points us to Jesus, our eternal source of help, while highlighting crucial biblical truths and promises we all need to cling to in the midst of our own hard things."

—LYSA TERKEURST, *NEW YORK TIMES* BESTSELLING AUTHOR OF *UNINVITED*; PRESIDENT, PROVERBS 31 MINISTRIES

"Hope is an increasingly scarce commodity these days. That's why I'm so grateful for Max Lucado's voice and for *Unshakable Hope*. For some people, this book will be a deeply needed reminder of what we already know about God, life, and the future but usually forget. For many others, it will be an introduction on how to finally beat cynicism and discouragement, something the world desperately needs."

—CAREY NIEUWHOF, FOUNDING PASTOR, CONNEXUS CHURCH

"Life doesn't turn out like we expect it to and hope is often in short supply. It's then that we have to decide what we will place our hope in. With pastoral care and the heart of a friend, Max points us back to the only lasting source of hope, the promises of God. This is a must-read for anyone struggling with purpose, wrestling with despair, or losing trust."

—MARK BATTERSON, *NEW YORK TIMES* BESTSELLING AUTHOR OF *THE CIRCLE MAKER*; LEAD PASTOR, NATIONAL COMMUNITY CHURCH

"God is able and willing to do mighty things through His people who believe Him. When we are at our weakest, God's unchanging promises to live in and through us are our lifeline. Max Lucado is a hero of the faith and a reliable guide to take us on this journey!"

—JENNIE ALLEN, AUTHOR OF *NOTHING TO PROVE*; FOUNDER AND VISIONARY, IF:GATHERING

"A conversation with a supervisor. The decision of a spouse or a child. An earthquake or a car accident. Almost every day, an unexpected event or unforeseen circumstance arises to remind us how shaky the world is. With the recent and tragic rise of suicide rates, it's clear that more than ever, people are desperate for an unshakable place to build their lives. I thank God for working through Pastor Max Lucado to give us this precious resource, brimming with Scripture-saturated hope, and leading us to the only unshakable foundation for life—the unfailing promises of God. *Unshakable Hope* will draw you closer to the God who promises to richly provide for all your needs, and will give you Scripture-based anchor points to hold you through life's storms. I hope you'll keep a copy close at hand in every season of life."

—LOUIE GIGLIO, PASTOR, PASSION CITY CHURCH; FOUNDER, PASSION CONFERENCES; AUTHOR OF *GOLIATH MUST FALL*

"Bangor, Maine, is a small town with only a few flights in and out per day yet it boasts an enormous international airport with a two-mile-long runway that can accommodate the largest planes in the world. The reason is strategic, Bangor is the first piece of American soil Atlantic flights hit after twenty-five hundred miles of water. If they are in distress they don't have to ditch in the ocean if they can just make it to Bangor. The book you hold in your hands offers for your soul what Bangor does for airplanes running on fumes: a safe place to land. Max Lucado does in his fortieth book what has earned him a place of trust in our hearts through the other thirty-nine—he points the way to the miles-long runway of God's unshakable hope that can handle the weight of your hurt."

—LEVI LUSKO, AUTHOR OF *I DECLARE WAR: 4 KEYS TO WINNING THE WAR WITH YOURSELF*

"In a world where despair and anxiety are at epidemic levels, Max reminds us that our sure and certain hope is found in the unchanging promises of God."

—SHEILA WALSH, AUTHOR OF *IT'S OKAY NOT TO BE OKAY*

UNSHAKABLE
HOPE

Also by Max Lucado

Inspirational

3:16

A Gentle Thunder

A Love Worth Giving

And the Angels Were Silent

Anxious for Nothing

Because of Bethlehem

Before Amen

Come Thirsty

Cure for the Common Life

Facing Your Giants

Fearless

Glory Days

God Came Near

Grace

Great Day Every Day

He Chose the Nails

He Still Moves Stones

In the Eye of the Storm

In the Grip of Grace

It's Not About Me

Just Like Jesus

Max on Life

More to Your Story

Next Door Savior

No Wonder They Call
Him the Savior

On the Anvil

Outlive Your Life

Six Hours One Friday

The Applause of Heaven

The Great House of God

Traveling Light

When Christ Comes

When God Whispers
Your Name

You'll Get Through This

Fiction

Christmas Stories

The Christmas Candle

Miracle at the Higher
Grounds Café

Bibles (General Editor)

Grace for the Moment
Daily Bible

The Lucado Life Lessons
Study Bible

Children's Daily
Devotional Bible

Children's Books

A Max Lucado
Children's Treasury

Do You Know I Love You, God?

God Forgives Me, and
I Forgive You

God Listens When I Pray

Grace for the Moment:
365 Devotions for Kids

Hermie, a Common Caterpillar

Itsy Bitsy Christmas

I'm Not a Scaredy Cat

Just in Case You Ever Wonder

Lucado Treasury of
Bedtime Prayers

One Hand, Two Hands

Thank You, God,
for Blessing Me

Thank You, God, for Loving Me

The Boy and the Ocean

The Crippled Lamb

The Oak Inside the Acorn

The Tallest of Smalls

You Are Mine

You Are Special

Young Adult Books

3:16

It's Not About Me

Make Every Day Count

Wild Grace

You Were Made to
Make a Difference

Gift Books

Fear Not Promise Book

For the Tough Times

God Thinks You're Wonderful

Grace for the Moment

Grace Happens Here

His Name Is Jesus

Let the Journey Begin

Live Loved

Mocha with Max

Safe in the Shepherd's Arms

This Is Love

You Changed My Life

UNSHAKABLE
HOPE

BUILDING OUR LIVES ON THE
PROMISES OF GOD

MAX LUCADO

THOMAS NELSON
Since 1798

Published in Nashville, Tennessee, by Thomas Nelson. Thomas Nelson is a registered trademark of HarperCollins Christian Publishing, Inc.

Thomas Nelson titles may be purchased in bulk for educational, business, fundraising, or sales promotional use. For information, please e-mail SpecialMarkets@ThomasNelson.com.

Unless otherwise noted, Scripture quotations are taken from the Holy Bible, New International Version®, NIV®. Copyright © 1973, 1978, 1984, 2011 by Biblica, Inc.™ Used by permission of Zondervan. All rights reserved worldwide. www.zondervan.com.

Other Scripture references are from the following sources: American Standard Version (ASV). English Standard Version (ESV), © 2001 by Crossway Bibles, a division of Good News Publishers. God's Word (GOD'S WORD) is a copyrighted work of God's Word to the Nations Bible Society. Quotations are used by permission. © 1995 by God's Word to the Nations Bible Society. All rights reserved. King James Version (KJV). *The Message* (THE MESSAGE). Copyright © by Eugene H. Peterson 1993, 1994, 1995, 1996, 2000, 2001, 2002. Used by permission of Tyndale House Publishers, Inc. New American Standard Bible® (NASB). Copyright © 1960, 1962, 1963, 1968, 1971, 1972, 1973, 1975, 1977, 1995 by The Lockman Foundation. Used by permission. (www.Lockman.org). New Century Version® (NCV). © 2005 by Thomas Nelson. Used by permission. All rights reserved. New King James Version® (NKJV). © 1982 by Thomas Nelson. Used by permission. All rights reserved. *Holy Bible,* New Living Translation (NLT). © 1996, 2004, 2007, 2013 by Tyndale House Foundation. Used by permission of Tyndale House Publishers, Inc., Carol Stream, Illinois 60188. All rights reserved. New Life Version (NLV). © Christian Literature International. J. B. Phillips: THE NEW TESTAMENT IN MODERN ENGLISH, Revised Edition (PHILLIPS). © J. B. Phillips 1958, 1960, 1972. Used by permission of Macmillan Publishing Co., Inc. Revised Standard Version of the Bible (RSV), copyright 1946, 1952, and 1971 National Council of the Churches of Christ in the United States of America. Used by permission. All rights reserved. *The Living Bible* (TLB). Copyright © 1971. Used by permission of Tyndale House Publishers, Inc., Carol Stream, Illinois 60188. All rights reserved.

ISBN: 978-1-4041-0804-2 (custom)
ISBN: 978-0-7180-9614-4 (HC)
ISBN: 978-1-4002-1212-5 (signed)
ISBN: 978-0-7180-7422-7 (IE)
ISBN: 978-0-7180-9645-8 (Ebook)

Library of Congress Control Number: 2018936435

Printed in the United States of America
18 19 20 21 22 LSC 6 5 4 3 2 1

For Mikal and Tammy Watts.
Your love and generosity remind us of Jesus.
We thank God for your unshakable faith and friendship.

He plunged into the promise and came up strong.

—Romans 4:20 THE MESSAGE

Contents

Acknowledgments   xiii

1. God's Great and Precious Promises   1
2. Stamped with God's Image   15
3. The Devil's Days Are Numbered   23
4. An Heir of God   35
5. Your Prayers Have Power   47
6. Grace for the Humble   57
7. God Gets You   69
8. Christ Is Praying for You   81
9. No Condemnation   91
10. This Temporary Tomb   103
11. Joy Is Soon Coming   115
12. You Will Have Power   127
13. Justice Will Prevail   141
14. Unbreakable Promises, Unshakable Hope   153

Questions for Reflection   167
Notes   213

Acknowledgments

Forty.

Noah floated for 40 days in the flood.

Moses spent 40 years in the desert.

The Hebrews wandered 40 years in the wilderness.

Jesus endured 40 days of temptation.

There's something significant about the number 40.

So, if you'll allow me to mention the fact, this is my fortieth book. No one could be more grateful than I am. To think that God would let a converted drunk prone to self-promotion and self-centeredness, write one page, much less forty books' worth, is yet another testimony to his goodness and grace.

Thank you, Father.

And thank you to this invaluable team of colleagues and friends.

- Karen Hill and Liz Heaney—editors who set the highest standard.
- Carol Bartley—incomparable copy editor.
- Steve and Cheryl Green—in some language your names mean "faithful and true." For indeed you are.

ACKNOWLEDGMENTS

- The HCCP superheroes: Mark Schoenwald, David Moberg, Brian Hampton, Mark Glesne, Jessalyn Foggy, LeeEric Fesko, Janene MacIvor, Debbie Nichols, and Laura Minchew.
- Brand team managers Greg and Susan Ligon. You could not possibly be more efficient. And I could not possibly be more grateful.
- Administrative assistants Janie Padilla and Margaret Mechinus. For all you do, thank you!
- The staff of the Oak Hills Church—we've learned to stand on promises together.
- Our splendid family—Brett, Jenna, Rosie and Max; Andrea; Jeff and Sara. No dad or grandpa could be prouder.
- And Denalyn, my dear wife.

  Had I the pen of a poet,
  had I the stars to give you,
  even then I couldn't show it,
  I couldn't show the love I have for you.

CHAPTER 1

God's Great and Precious Promises

GOD'S PROMISE

[God] has given us his very great and
precious promises, so that through them
you may participate in the divine nature.

—2 Peter 1:4

The contrast between the rabbi and the king was stark. The Jew was old and bent. He had no bodily advantage. Two years in prison had left him gaunt, his cheeks hollow and smudged. His purse had but a few coins and his entourage but a couple of friends. Baldness laureled his head. His beard was full yet gray. He wore the simple cloak of a teacher, a traveling teacher. Compared to the king, he was simple, impoverished. Of course, compared to this king, most people were simple and impoverished. King Agrippa entered the court that day with great pomp. He and his sister were arrayed in purple. Roman legionnaires followed. Agrippa was the appointed ruler, the curator of religion, and the overseer of the area.

Paul, by contrast, was a simple missionary. He had every reason to fear the judgment of this monarch. The king was the latest in the Herod dynasty, the last of the Herods who would meddle with Christ or his followers. His great-grandfather attempted to kill baby Jesus by slaughtering the children of Bethlehem. His granduncle murdered John the Baptist, and his father, Agrippa I, executed James and imprisoned Peter.

You might say they had it out for the people in Jesus' circle.

And now Paul stood before him. He was in prison, and in trouble, for preaching a new religion. How would the apostle defend himself? Appeal for mercy? Call for a miracle? In what was arguably the most important speech of his life, how would Paul present his case? After a word of introduction, he said, "And now it is because of my hope in what God has promised our ancestors that I am on trial today" (Acts 26:6).

Paul's defense included no reference to his accomplishments.

("I have been known to call a person back from the dead, you know.") He demanded no preferential treatment. ("I am a Roman citizen.") He didn't attempt to justify his actions. ("I was only being open-minded.") None of that. His only justification was this: "I believed in the promises of God."

So did Abraham and Isaac and Jacob. Add to that list Noah, Mary, a prophet named Isaiah, and a preacher named Peter.

The heroes in the Bible came from all walks of life: rulers, servants, teachers, doctors. They were male, female, single, and married. Yet one common denominator united them: they built their lives on the promises of God. Because of God's promises, Noah believed in rain before *rain* was a word. Because of God's promises, Abraham left a good home for one he'd never seen. Because of God's promises, Joshua led two million people into enemy territory. Because of God's promises, David conked a giant, Peter rose from the ashes of regret, and Paul found a grace worth dying for.

One writer went so far as to call such saints "heirs of the promise" (Heb. 6:17 NASB). It is as if the promise was the family fortune, and they were smart enough to attend the reading of the will.

> By faith Noah, when warned about things not yet seen, in holy fear built an ark to save his family. . . .
>
> By faith Abraham, when called to go to a place he would later receive as his inheritance, obeyed and went, even though he did not know where he was going. . . . He lived in tents, as did Isaac and Jacob, who were heirs with him of the same promise. . . . And by faith even Sarah, who was past childbearing age, was enabled to bear children because she considered him faithful who had made the promise. . . .
>
> By faith Abraham, when God tested him, offered Isaac as a sacrifice. He who had embraced the promises was about to sacrifice his one and only son. (Heb. 11:7–17)

The list goes on for several verses. Jacob trusted God's promises. Joseph trusted God's promises. Moses trusted God's promises. Their stories were different, but the theme was the same: God's promises were polestars in their pilgrimages of faith. They had plenty of promises from which to pick.

One student of Scripture spent a year and a half attempting to tally the number of promises God has made to humanity. He came up with 7,487 promises![1] God's promises are pine trees in the Rocky Mountains of Scripture: abundant, unbending, and perennial. Some of the promises are positive, the assurance of blessings. Some are negative, the guarantee of consequences. But all are binding, for not only is God a promise maker; God is a promise keeper.

As God was preparing the Israelites to face a new land, he made a promise to them.

> Then the LORD said: "I am making a covenant with you. Before all your people I will do wonders never before done in any nation in all the world. The people you live among will see how awesome is the work that I, the LORD, will do for you." (Ex. 34:10)

God did not emphasize the Israelites' strength. He emphasized his. He did not underscore their ability. He highlighted his. He equipped them for the journey by headlining his capacity to make and keep his promises.

From the first chapter of Scripture, the Bible makes a case for the dependability of God. Nine times the text reiterates "God said." And without exception when God spoke, something happened. Something wonderful happened. By divine fiat there was light, land, beaches, and creatures. God consulted no advisers. He needed no assistance. He spoke, and it happened. The reader is left with one conclusion: God's word is sure. What he says happens.

By the word of the LORD the heavens were made,

their starry host by the breath of his mouth.

He gathers the waters of the sea into jars;

he puts the deep into storehouses.

Let all the earth fear the LORD;

let all the people of the world revere him.

For he spoke, and it came to be;

he commanded, and it stood firm. (Ps. 33:6–9)

When God cleared his throat, the cosmos appeared. His authority was certain.

The same power is seen in Jesus Christ. On one occasion an officer in the Roman military asked Jesus to heal his servant. Jesus offered to go to the man's home. The officer refused, saying,

"Lord, I do not deserve to have you come under my roof. But just say the word, and my servant will be healed. For I myself am a man under authority, with soldiers under me. I tell this one, 'Go,' and he goes; and that one, 'Come,' and he comes. I say to my servant, 'Do this,' and he does it."

When Jesus heard this, he was amazed and said to those following him, "Truly I tell you, I have not found anyone in Israel with such great faith. . . ."

Then Jesus said to the centurion, "Go! Let it be done just as you believed it would." And his servant was healed at that moment. (Matt. 8:8–10, 13)

Why did Jesus applaud the faith of the centurion? Because the man believed in the power of Jesus to keep his word. In fact, this story gives us Jesus' definition of faith: *faith is the deeply held belief that God will keep his promises.* The Roman soldier understood this simple truth: God will not—indeed he cannot—break his promises. His covenants are contractually inviolable, written not in sand but carved in granite. What he says will happen.

It must happen! His promises are irrevocable because of who God is:

- He is unchanging. He sees the end from the beginning. He's never caught off guard by the unexpected. He makes no midcourse corrections. He is not victimized by moods or weather. "He never changes or casts a shifting shadow" (James 1:17 NLT).
- He is faithful. "God can be trusted to keep his promise" (Heb. 10:23 NLT).
- He is strong. He does not overpromise and underdeliver. "God is able to do whatever he promises" (Rom. 4:21 NLT).
- He cannot lie. "It is impossible for God to lie" (Heb. 6:18 NLT). A rock cannot swim. A hippo cannot fly. A butterfly cannot eat a bowl of spaghetti. You cannot sleep on a cloud, and God cannot lie. He never exaggerates, manipulates, fibs, or flatters. This verse does not say it is unlikely that God will lie or improbable that God will lie. No, the statement is clear: it is impossible! Scripture could not be more forthright. "God . . . cannot lie" (Titus 1:2 ASV). Deceit is simply not an option. "He doesn't break promises!" (Titus 1:2 THE MESSAGE).

This theme of God as a promise keeper stirs a childhood memory. When I was around twelve years old, I tagged along with my father as he went to buy new tires for the family car. Dad was from a small town and simpler times. He was unadorned of fancy dress or wealth. He was a reliable oil field mechanic who loved his family, paid his bills, and kept his word. He was insulted by those who doubted his integrity. He was certainly insulted that day in the tire shop.

He selected the tires, and we waited as they were being mounted. When it came time to pay the bill, I stood by Dad's side at the counter as he wrote the check. The salesclerk looked at the check and then requested that my father produce some identification. Such a practice is common and unquestioned today, but in the 1960s a merchant seldom asked for verification.

Dad was taken aback.

"You don't believe I am who that check says I am?"

The clerk was embarrassed. "We require this of all customers."

"Do you think I am dishonest?"

"It's not that, sir."

"If you don't think I am good for my word, you can remove those tires."

I remember a long moment of awkward silence as the clerk weighed his options.

We went home with the tires. And I went home with a lesson on integrity. Good people are serious about keeping their word. How much more serious would a good God be? What was said about God's faithfulness to Israel can be said about his faithfulness to us. "Not one of all the LORD's good promises to Israel failed; every one was fulfilled" (Josh. 21:45).

The question is not, will God keep his promises, but, will we build our lives upon them?

I have many quirks, not the least of which is a shaky left thumb. For the last decade or so, it has quivered. It's as if my thumb lives on a caffeine drip. Were I to secure a glass of soda left-handed, I would slosh it everywhere. But I'm not left-handed, so the quiver doesn't bother me. I actually use it as a conversation starter. ("Hey, can I show you my shaky thumb? Now you show me your oddities.")

I've grown accustomed to the localized tremor. At first, however, I wasn't so calm. The shaking shook me. I thought something had come unwired. Because my father passed away from ALS, my imagination assumed the worse. The situation was especially unnerving because my left thumb follows me everywhere I go. When I comb my hair, there's Old Wobbly. When I putt, guess who can't settle down? If I raise my left hand to make a point in a sermon, you might not trust what I say because of the knockety knuckle.

I set up an appointment with the neurologist and entered his office with a dry mouth and dread. He reviewed my blood work and examined me. He had me walk, balance, and spin a few plates on my finger. (Just kidding. He didn't make me walk.) He tapped my knee with a rubber hammer and asked me some questions. Then after an interminably long time, he said, "No need to worry."

"You sure?"

"I'm sure."

"No treatment?"

"Nope."

"No wheelchair?"

"Nope, not from what I can see."

"You sure?"

He then did something profound. "I promise," he assured me. "The tremor in your thumb is nothing to worry about."

So I hopped down and thanked him and walked out. I felt better. I climbed in the car and began the drive home. While stopped at a traffic light, I noticed my left hand on the steering wheel. Can you guess what my thumb was doing? Yep. It was shaking.

For the first time since the tremor had appeared, I had the opportunity to look at it differently. I could ponder the problem, or I could remember the promise. I could choose anxiety, or I could choose hope. I opted for hope. As corny as this might sound, I can remember saying to my thumb, "You're not getting any more of my attention. The doctor made me a promise. You are harmless." From that moment on, each time the thumb has misbehaved, I've thought of the promise from the doctor.

What is shaking in your world? Not likely your thumb, but possibly your future, your faith, your family, or your finances. It's a shaky world out there.

Could you use some unshakable hope?

If so, you are not alone. We live in a day of despair. The suicide rate in America has increased 24 percent since 1999.[2] Twenty-four percent! If a disease saw such a spike, we would deem it an epidemic. How do we explain the increase? We've never been more educated. We have tools of technology our parents could not have dreamed of. We are saturated with entertainment and recreation. Yet more people than ever are orchestrating their own deaths. How could this be?

Among the answers must be this: people are dying for lack of hope. Secularism sucks the hope out of society. It reduces the world to a few decades between birth and hearse. Many people believe this world is as good as it gets, and let's face it. It's not that good.

But People of the Promise have an advantage. They determine to ponder, proclaim, and pray the promises of God. They are like Abraham who "didn't tiptoe around God's promise asking cautiously skeptical questions. He plunged into the promise and came up strong" (Rom. 4:20 THE MESSAGE).

They filter life through the promises of God. When problems surface, they can be heard telling themselves, "But God said . . ." When struggles threaten, they can be seen flipping through Scripture, saying, "I think God said something about this." When comforting others, they're prone to ask, "Do you know God's promise on this topic?"

The promises of God serve as an apothecary shelf of remedies. Just as the doctor might prescribe a medication for your body, God has given promises for your heart. He shares them as gifts from friend to friend. "Friendship with God is reserved for those who reverence him. With them alone he shares the secrets of his promises" (Ps. 25:14 TLB).

For every problem in life God has given us a promise. Make it your aim to get so acquainted with these promises that you can write yourself a prescription.

- I'm feeling fearful today. Time for me to open up a bottle of Judges 6:12: "The LORD is with you." I will lay claim to the nearness of God.
- The world feels out of control. Time for a dose of Romans 8:28: "All things work together for good" (NKJV).
- I see dark clouds on the horizon. What was it Jesus told me? Oh, now I remember: "In this world you will have trouble. But take heart! I have overcome the world" (John 16:33).

After forty (!) years of ministry I've discovered that nothing lifts the weary soul like the promises of God. This book contains some of my favorites. Many of them are go-to promises I've turned to throughout the years to encourage others. And to encourage myself. We desperately need them. We do not need more opinions or hunches; we need the definitive declarations of our mighty and loving God. He governs the world according to these great and precious promises.

The circumstances of life or the promises of God—upon which are you standing?

Jesus told a story about two home builders. They had similar supplies and plans and identical aspirations. Each wanted to build a house. But one preferred the cheap and easily accessed land of sand. The other opted for the more expensive yet more durable foundation of stone.

Therefore everyone who hears these words of mine and puts them into practice is like a wise man who built his house on the rock.

The rain came down, the streams rose, and the winds blew and beat against that house; yet it did not fall, because it had its foundation on the rock. But everyone who hears these words of mine and does not put them into practice is like a foolish man who built his house on sand. The rain came down, the streams rose, and the winds blew and beat against that house, and it fell with a great crash. (Matt. 7:24–27)

What separates the wise from the foolish? Both men hear God's words. But only the wise man builds his house upon them.

How is your foundation holding up? I wonder if a modern-day version of the parable might read like this:

Two people set out to build their houses. The first went to RPF Home Supply: Regrets, Pain, and Fear. He ordered lumber that was rotted by guilt, nails that were rusty from pain, and cement that was watered down with anxiety. Since his home was constructed with RPF supplies, every day was consumed with regret, pain, and fear.

The second builder chose a different supplier. She secured her supplies from Hope Incorporated. Rather than choose regret, pain, and fear, she found ample promises of grace, protection, and security. She made the deliberate, conscious decision to build a life from the storehouse of hope.

Which of the two builders was wiser? Which of the two was happier? Which of the two is most like you?

By the way, I'm standing on a promise as I share these words.

As the rain and snow come down from heaven and stay upon the ground to water the earth, and cause the grain to grow and to produce seed for the farmer and bread for the hungry, so also is my word. I send it out, and it always produces fruit. It shall accomplish all I want it to and prosper everywhere I send it. (Isa. 55:10–11 TLB)

Note the certainty of God's promise. God's word "always produces fruit. It shall accomplish all I want it to and prosper everywhere I send it."

Picture God's words falling like rain from heaven on you. Imagine these promises as gentle spring showers. Receive them. Allow them to land on you, to soak you. I'm trusting that God's words will prosper in your life. Will you join me in believing this promise?

According to Peter, God's promises aren't just great; they are "very great." They aren't just valuable; they are "precious" (2 Peter 1:4). To bind them around your neck is to adorn yourself with the finest jewels of the universe. It is through the *great and precious promises* that we participate in the divine nature of God. They lead us into a new reality, a holy environment. They are direction signs intended to guide us away from the toxic swampland and into the clean air of heaven. They sit like golden stones in the pathway to God's world. They are strong boulders that form the bridge over which we walk from our sin to salvation. Promises are the stitching in the spine of the Bible.

The American evangelist Dwight Moody said it this way:

Let a man feed for a month on the promises of God, and he will not talk about his poverty. . . . If you would only go from Genesis to Revelation and see all the promises made by God to Abraham, to Isaac, to Jacob, to the Jews and the Gentiles, and to all His people everywhere; if you would spend a month feeding on the precious promises of God, you would not go about . . . complaining about how poor you are, but you would lift up your heads with confidence and proclaim the riches of His Grace, because you could not help it.[3]

Let's be what we were made to be—People of the Promise. Keep this declaration handy. Say it out loud. Fill your lungs with air and your heart with hope, and let the devil himself hear you declare your belief in God's goodness.

We are building our lives on the promises of God.
Because his Word is unbreakable, our hope is unshakable.
We do not stand on the problems of life or the pain in life.
We stand on the great and precious promises of God.

CHAPTER 2

Stamped with God's Image

GOD'S PROMISE

Let us make human beings in our image,
make them reflecting our nature.

—Genesis 1:26 THE MESSAGE

Sometime ago I videotaped a message for our church. We recruited a film crew and drove to the Alamo. We selected a park bench in front of the shrine of Texas liberty, set up the equipment, and got busy.

Four workers managed sight and sound with lights and cameras. I sat on the bench, trying to remember my thoughts. We must have looked official. Passersby began to pause; some started to stare. *Who is that guy? What are they filming?*

One woman's curiosity erupted into a question that she shouted at me from behind the crew. "Are you somebody important?"

Every soul on earth has asked the same question. Not about a redhead on a park bench, mind you, but about themselves.

Am I somebody important?

It's easy to feel anything but important when the corporation sees you as a number, the boyfriend treats you like cattle, your ex takes your energy, or old age takes your dignity. Somebody important? Hardly.

When you struggle with that question, remember this promise of God: you were created by God, in God's image, for God's glory.

> God spoke: "Let us make human beings in our image, make them
> reflecting our nature
> So they can be responsible for the fish in the sea,
> the birds in the air, the cattle,
> And, yes, Earth itself,
> and every animal that moves on the face of Earth." (Gen. 1:26
> THE MESSAGE)

Embedded in these words is the most wonderful of promises: God made us to reflect the image of God.

God created us to be more like him than anything else he made. He never declared, "Let us make oceans in our image" or "birds in our likeness." The heavens above reflect the glory of God, but they are not made in the image of God. Yet we are.

To be clear: no one is a god except in his or her own delusion. But everyone carries some of the communicable attributes of God. Wisdom. Love. Grace. Kindness. A longing for eternity. These are just some of the attributes that set us apart from the farm animal and suggest that we bear the fingerprints of the Divine Maker. We are made in *his image* and in *his likeness*.

These terms self-define a few chapters later. "When Adam had lived 130 years, he had a son in his own likeness, in his own image; and he named him Seth" (Gen. 5:3). Seth bore the image and likeness of his father. Maybe he had his father's curly hair or dark eyes. Apart from having a belly button, Seth was like Adam in many ways.

The same is true of us. We "take after" God in many ways. There is no exception to this promise. Every man and woman, born or preborn, rich or poor, urban or rural, is made in the image of God. Some suppress it. Others enhance it. But all were made in the image of God.

Sin has distorted this image, but it has not destroyed it. Our moral purity has been tainted. Our intellect is polluted by foolish ideas. We have fallen prey to the elixir of self-promotion rather than God-promotion. The image of God is sometimes difficult to discern. But do not think for a moment that God has rescinded his promise or altered his plan. He still creates people in his image to bear his likeness and reflect his glory.

The New Testament describes a progressive work of God to shape us into his image. As we fellowship with God, read his Word, obey his commands, and seek to understand and reflect his character, something wonderful emerges. Or, better stated, *Someone* wonderful emerges. God comes out of us. We say things God would say. We do things God would do. We forgive, we share, and we love. It is as if God is scrubbing the smudge off an old coin. In time an image begins to appear.

God's goal is simply this: to rub away anything that is not of him so the inborn image of God can be seen in us.

This was God's explanation through the apostle Paul.

You have taken off your old self with its practices and have put on the new self, which is being renewed in knowledge in the image of its Creator. (Col. 3:9–10)

We . . . are being transformed into his image with ever-increasing glory, which comes from the Lord, who is the Spirit. (2 Cor. 3:18)

Pop psychology is wrong when it tells you to look inside yourself and find your value. The magazines are wrong when they suggest you are only as good as you are thin, muscular, pimple-free, or perfumed. The movies mislead you when they imply that your value increases as your stamina, intelligence, or net worth grows. Religious leaders lie when they urge you to grade your significance according to your church attendance, self-discipline, or spirituality.

According to the Bible you are good simply because God made you in his image. Period. He cherishes you because you bear a resemblance to him. And you will only be satisfied when you engage in your role as an image bearer of God. Such was the view of King David: "As for me, I will see Your face in righteousness; I shall be satisfied when I awake in Your likeness" (Ps. 17:15 NKJV).

Lay hold of this promise, and spare yourself a world of confusion and fear. How much sadness would evaporate if every person simply chose to believe this: *I was made for God's glory and am being made into his image.*

As I was about to sit down and review this chapter, my daughter Jenna stepped into my office. She is as round as a ladybug. In six weeks she will, God willing, give birth to a baby girl. Can I tell you something about that infant? I love her. I've never seen her, but I love her. She has done nothing to earn my love. But I love her. She's never brought me coffee or called me Papa. She's never sung me a song or danced me a dance. She has done nothing!

Yet I love her already.

I would do anything for her, and that is not hyperbole.

Why? Why do I love her so? Because she carries some of me. A small part for sure but a part of me nonetheless.

Why does God love you with an everlasting love? It has nothing to do with you. It has everything to do with whose you are. You are his. You carry a part of him. There is something of him in you. He made you in his image. He stamped his name on your heart. He breathed life into your lungs.

Someone called you a lost cause. Someone branded you as a failure. Someone dismissed you as insignificant. Don't listen to them. They don't know what they are talking about. A divine spark indwells you. When you say yes to God, he blows on that holy ember, and it begins to flame. It grows day by day within you. Are you perfect? No. But you are being made perfect. He bought you and owns you and has a wild and inexplicable love for you. His love for you does not depend on you.

You are God's idea. God's child. Created in God's image.

Would you let this truth find its way into your heart? You were conceived by God before you were conceived by your parents. You were loved in heaven before you were known on earth. You aren't an accident. You aren't a random fluke of genetics or evolution. You aren't defined by the number of pounds you weigh, followers you have, car you drive, or clothes you wear.

CEO or unemployed—doesn't matter.
Hot list or not list—doesn't matter.
Blue-blooded or orphaned—doesn't matter.
High IQ or low standing—doesn't matter.
First string or cut from the squad—doesn't matter.

You are being made into God's image. Print that on your résumé. You are a diamond, a rose, and a jewel, purchased by the blood of Jesus Christ. In the eyes of God you are worth dying for. Would you let this truth define the way you see yourself?

Would you let this truth define the way you see other people? Every person you see was created by God to bear his image and deserves to be treated with dignity and respect. This means *all* people deserve to be seen for who they are: image bearers of God.

Imagine the impact this promise would have on the society that embraced it. What civility it would engender! What kindness it would foster! Racism will not flourish when people believe their neighbors bear God's image. The fire of feuds will have no fuel when people believe their adversaries are God's idea. Will a man abuse a woman? Not if he believes she bears the stamp of God. Will a boss neglect an employee? Not if she believes the employee bears a divine spark. Will society write off the indigent, the mentally ill, the inmate on death row, or the refugee? Not if we believe, truly believe, that every human being is God's idea. And he has no bad ideas.

You and I were made by God to know him and make him known.

Children have a tendency to say, "Look at me!" On the tricycle: "Look at me go!" On the trampoline: "Look at me bounce!" On the swing set: "Look at me swing!" Such behavior is acceptable for children.

Yet many adults spend their grown-up years saying the same. "Look at me drive this fancy car!" "Look at me make money!" "Look at me wear provocative clothes, use big words, or flex my muscles. Look at me!"

Isn't it time we grew up? We were made to live a life that says, "Look at God!" People are to look at us and see not us but the image of our Maker.

This is God's plan. This is God's promise. And he will fulfill it! He will make us into his image.

CHAPTER 3

The Devil's Days Are Numbered

GOD'S PROMISE

The God who brings peace will soon defeat
Satan and give you power over him.

—Romans 16:20 NCV

The thought of the picnickers doesn't surprise us. The people weren't the first or the last to pack a meal and set out for a Sunday afternoon excursion. After all, it was a quiet and sunny July day. A trip to the countryside would be nice. No, it wasn't the picnic baskets that made this entourage notable. It is where they went to unpack them.

A battlefield. On July 21, 1861, Washingtonians rode horses and buggies to Manassas to witness their Union soldiers bring an end to what they considered to be a short rebellion. Their intent was to sit on blankets, eat their chicken, and cheer from a distance.

One soldier described them as a "throng of sightseers. . . . They came in all manner of ways, some in stylish carriages, others in city hacks, and still others in buggies, on horseback and even on foot. . . . It was Sunday and everybody seemed to have taken a general holiday."[1]

A reporter from the *London Times* observed, "The spectators were all excited, and a lady with an opera glass . . . was quite beside herself [at the sound of] an unusually heavy discharge. . . . 'That is splendid, Oh my! Is not that first rate?'"[2]

It wasn't long before reality rushed in. With the sound of gunfire, the sight of blood, and the screams of wounded soldiers, people soon realized this was no picnic. Fathers grabbed their children, and husbands called for their wives. They jumped into their wagons and onto their horses. Some were "caught in a stampede of retreating Union troops."[3] One spectator, a congressman from New York, was caught by Confederate soldiers and kept prisoner for nearly six months.[4]

That was the last time onlookers took picnic baskets to a battle-field. Or was it?

Could it be that we make a similar mistake? Could it be that we embrace a similar false assumption? Is it possible we do today what the Washingtonians did then? According to the Bible, we're in a war that's a-raging.

> Our fight is not against people on earth but against the rulers and authorities and the powers of this world's darkness, against the spiritual powers of evil in the heavenly world. That is why you need to put on God's full armor. Then on the day of evil you will be able to stand strong. And when you have finished the whole fight, you will still be standing. So stand strong, with the belt of truth tied around your waist and the protection of right living on your chest. On your feet wear the Good News of peace to help you stand strong. And also use the shield of faith with which you can stop all the burning arrows of the Evil One. (Eph. 6:12–16 NCV)

The Bible names a real and present foe of our faith: the devil. The Greek word for "devil" is *diabolos*, and it shares a root with the verb *diaballein*, which means "to split."[5] The devil is a splitter, a divider, a wedge driver. He divided Adam and Eve from God in the garden and would like to separate you from God as well. He wants to take unbelievers to hell and make life hell for believers.

Do such thoughts sound outdated? Do you file discussions of the devil in the manila folder labeled "superstition" or "antiquated religion"? If so, you aren't alone. According to the research of the Barna Group, "Four out of ten Christians (40%) strongly agreed that Satan 'is not a living being but is a symbol of evil.' An additional two out of ten Christians (19%) said they 'agree somewhat' with that perspective. A minority of Christians [35%] indicated that they believe Satan is real. . . . The remaining [participants] were not sure what they believe about the existence of Satan."[6]

Most Christians, in other words, refuse to believe in the existence of Satan.

Surely the current ridicule and skepticism with which he is viewed must please him deeply. As long as he isn't taken seriously, he is free to work his evil. After all, if you can't diagnose the source of your ills, how can you fight them? The devil wants to make your life a mess and to keep his name out of it.

But God doesn't let him do so.

The Bible traces Satan's activities to a moment of rebellion that occurred sometime between the creation of the universe and the appearance of the snake in the garden. When God created the world, "God saw all that he had made, and it was very good" (Gen. 1:31). In the beginning everything was good. Every drop of water, every tree, every animal, and, by extension, every angel. Yet sometime between the events described in Genesis 1 and those described in Genesis 3, an angel led a coup against God and was cast from heaven. The prophet Ezekiel described the downfall.

This is what the Sovereign LORD says:

> "You were the seal of perfection,
>   full of wisdom and perfect in beauty.
> You were in Eden,
>   the garden of God;
>
> You were anointed as a guardian cherub,
>   for so I ordained you.
> You were on the holy mount of God;
>   you walked among the fiery stones.

> You were blameless in your ways
>> from the day you were created
>> till wickedness was found in you." (Ezek. 28:12–15)

To whom God was speaking? This being

- was in Eden,
- was anointed as a guardian angel,
- dwelt on God's holy mountain, and
- was blameless from the day he was made until the day wickedness appeared.

Who could this be but Satan? This prophecy is nothing less than a description of the fall of the devil.

> Through your widespread trade
>> you were filled with violence,
>> and you sinned.
> So I drove you in disgrace from the mount of God,
>> and I expelled you, guardian cherub,
>> from among the fiery stones.
> Your heart became proud
>> on account of your beauty,
> and you corrupted your wisdom
>> because of your splendor.
> So I threw you to the earth;
>> I made a spectacle of you before kings. (vv. 16–17)

Lucifer's heart became proud. He was not content to worship; he had to be worshipped (Isa. 14:12–15). He was not content to bow before God's throne; he had to sit upon it. No wonder pride is a sin

God hates (Prov. 6:16–17; 8:13). No wonder Paul urged Timothy not to be too quick to promote a new convert "or he may become conceited and fall under the same judgment as the devil" (1 Tim. 3:6).

Satan succumbed to pride, and as a result he was cast out of heaven. Jesus referred to that eviction, saying, "I saw Satan fall like lightning from heaven" (Luke 10:18). When lightning falls, the descent is brief and electric. When Satan fell, his descent was the same.

But though he is cast out of heaven, he is not out of our lives. "Be alert and of sober mind. Your enemy the devil prowls around like a roaring lion looking for someone to devour" (1 Peter 5:8). He comes "only to steal and kill and destroy" (John 10:10). You're enjoying happiness? Satan wants to steal it. You've discovered joy? He'll try to kill it. Love your spouse? Satan would love to destroy your marriage. He is the enemy of your God-given destiny and longs to be the destroyer of your soul.

Don't dismiss him.

Agree with the witness of Scripture. From the Bible's first to final pages, we are confronted with an arrogant, anti-God force of great cunning and power. He is the devil, the serpent, the strong one, the lion, the wicked one, the accuser, the god of this age, the murderer, the prince of this world, the prince of the power of the air, Beelzebub, and Belial. He oversees a conglomeration of spiritual forces: principalities, powers, dominions, thrones, princes, lords, gods, angels, unclean and wicked spirits.

Satan appears in the garden at the beginning. He is cast into the fire in the end. He tempted David, bewildered Saul, and waged an attack on Job. He is in the Gospels, the book of Acts, the writings of Paul, Peter, John, James, and Jude. Serious students of Scripture must be serious about Satan.

Jesus was. He squared off against Satan in the wilderness (Matt. 4:1–11). He pegged Satan as the one who snatches the good news from the hearts of the hearers (Mark 4:15; Matt. 13:19). Prior to the cru-cifixion Jesus proclaimed, "Now shall the ruler of this world be cast out" (John 12:31 RSV). Jesus saw Satan not as a mythological image, not an invention of allegory. He saw the devil as a superhuman narcissist. When Jesus taught us to pray, he did not say, "Deliver us from nebulous negative emotions." He said, "Deliver us from the evil one" (Matt. 6:13).

We play into the devil's hand when we pretend he does not exist. The devil is a real devil.

But, and this is huge, *the devil is a defeated devil.* Were Satan to read the Bible (something he won't do), he would be utterly discouraged. Reference after reference makes this clear: the devil's days are numbered.

"Having disarmed the powers and authorities, [Jesus] made a public spectacle of [the forces of evil], triumphing over them by the cross" (Col. 2:15). Jesus stripped Satan of certain victory. He and his minions are being held on a short leash until the final judgment. On that day, the great Day, Jesus will cast Satan into a lake of fire from which the devil will never return (2 Peter 2:4; Jude v. 6). Evil will have its day and appear to have the sway, but God will have his say and ultimately win the day.

My friend Carter Conlon has ministered in New York City for more than two decades. Yet he spent many of his early years on a farm. He recalls a barnyard scene that illustrates the status of Satan. A fam-ily of cats lived in the barn. The mama cat would often be spotted in the field with a mouse. She would taunt and tease it until the mouse was exhausted. She would then bring the rodent to the kittens to teach them how to catch and kill it. Carter remembers how the mouse, upon seeing the kittens, would rise up on its hind feet and prepare to fight. The rodent would bare its tiny yellow teeth and flare its little claws. It would then attempt to hiss. Its only hope was to convince the kittens it was something other than what it was: a defeated, wimpy, outnumbered mouse. It had already lost. The kittens didn't even have to fight to win the victory.[7]

Jesus has already defeated the rat of heaven as well. Be alert to the devil, but don't be intimidated by him. Learn to recognize his stench. Since he comes to steal, kill, and destroy (John 10:10), wherever you see heists, death, and destruction, turn to God in prayer. Since his name means "divider," wherever you see divorce, rejection, and isolation, you know the culprit. Go immediately to Scripture. Stand on the promises of God regarding Satan:

> The God who brings peace will soon defeat Satan and give you power over him. (Rom. 16:20 NCV)

> God's Spirit, who is in you, is greater than the devil, who is in the world. (1 John 4:4 NCV)

> God is faithful; he will not let you be tempted beyond what you can bear. (1 Cor. 10:13)

> Resist the devil, and he will flee from you. (James 4:7)

> [The devil] is filled with fury,
> because he knows that his time is short. (Rev. 12:12)

> Put on God's full armor . . . with the belt of truth tied around your waist and the protection of right living on your chest. On your feet wear the Good News of peace to help you stand strong. And also use the shield of faith with which you can stop all the burning arrows of the Evil One. (Eph. 6:13–16 NCV)

Soldiers know better than to saunter onto the battlefield wearing nothing but shorts and sandals. They take care to prepare. They take every weapon into the conflict.

So must we! Every conflict is a contest with Satan and his forces. For that reason "though we walk in the flesh, we do not war according to the flesh. For the weapons of our warfare are not carnal but mighty in God for pulling down strongholds" (2 Cor. 10:3–4 NKJV).

What are these weapons? Prayer, worship, and Scripture. When we pray, we engage the power of God against the devil. When we worship, we do what Satan himself did not do: we place God on the throne. When we pick up the sword of Scripture, we do what Jesus did in the wilderness. He responded to Satan by proclaiming truth. And since Satan has a severe allergy to truth, he left Jesus alone.

Satan will not linger long where God is praised and prayers are offered.

Satan may be vicious, but he will not be victorious.

On several occasions I have known the name of the victor before the end of the contest. Being a pastor, I'm often unable to watch the Sunday football games. While I am preaching, the teams are playing. I don't complain, however, since I can always record the games. So I do.

Yet on many Sundays a well-wishing parishioner will receive a text or e-mail and learn the outcome of the game and feel the burden to share it with me. I've considered wearing a sign that reads "Recording the game. Don't tell me anything!"

I remember one contest in particular. My beloved Dallas Cowboys were playing a must-win game. I'd been careful to set the recorder and was looking forward to an afternoon of first downs and touchdowns. I avoided any mention of the event. I even avoided eye contact with anyone I thought might spill the beans. I made it as far as my car in the parking lot when an enthusiastic fan shouted out to me, "Max, did you hear the news? The Cowboys won!!!"

Grrr.

Gone was the suspense. Gone was the edge-of-the-seat anxiety. Gone was the nail biting and eye ducking. Even though I knew the outcome, I still wanted to watch the game. As I did, I made a delight-ful discovery. I could watch stress-free! The Cowboys fell behind in the second quarter, but I didn't worry. I knew the outcome. We fumbled the ball with six minutes to play. I didn't panic. I knew the winner. We needed a touchdown in the final minute. No problem. The victory was certain.

So is yours. Between now and the final whistle, you will have rea-son to be anxious. You are going to fumble the ball. The devil will seem to gain the upper hand. Some demon will intercept your dreams and destiny. All that is good will appear to lose. But you do not need to worry. You and I know the final score.

The next time you smell his stinky breath, remind him of the promise he is loath to hear: "The God who brings peace will soon defeat Satan and give you power over him" (Rom. 16:20 NCV).

It's a battle, so don't pack a picnic basket.

Yet it is a battle God has won, so don't give the devil more than a passing glance.

CHAPTER 4

An Heir of God

GOD'S PROMISE

We are heirs—heirs of God and co-heirs with Christ.

—Romans 8:17

The sixty-year-old body of Timothy Henry Gray was found under a Wyoming overpass two days after Christmas in 2012. There was no sign of foul play. No indication of a crime or mischief. A homeless cowboy who had died of hypothermia, Gray was a victim of bad breaks and bad luck.

Except for this detail: he stood to inherit millions of dollars.

Gray's great-grandfather was a wealthy copper miner, railroad builder, and the founder of a small Nevada town you might have heard of: Las Vegas. His fortune was passed down to his daughter, Huguette. She died in 2011 at the age of 104.

Huguette left a $300 million fortune. At the time of Gray's death, the execution of the will was tied up in court. As things turned out, the man found dead under the railroad overpass wasn't poor after all. He may have been worth $19 million.[1]

How does the heir to a fortune die like a pauper? Surely Timothy Gray knew his family history. Was he in touch with his half great-aunt? Did it ever occur to him to investigate a potential inheritance?

It would occur to me! I would camp on the doorstep of my dear great-aunt. I would turn over every stone and read every document. Wouldn't you? We'd make it our aim to access our inheritance, wouldn't we?

But do we?

Let's talk about yours. Glistening in the jewel box of God's promises to you is a guarantee of your inheritance: you are an heir—an heir of God and coheir with Christ (Rom. 8:17).

You aren't merely a slave, servant, or saint of God. No, you are a child of God. You have legal right to the family business and fortune of heaven. The will has been executed. The courts have been satisfied. Your spiritual account has been funded. He "has blessed [you] with every spiritual blessing in the heavenly places in Christ" (Eph. 1:3 NKJV).

You have everything you need to be everything God desires. Divine resources have been deposited in you.

Need more patience? It's yours.

Need more joy? Ask for it.

Running low on wisdom? God has plenty. Put in your order.

Your father is rich! "Yours, O LORD, is the greatness, the power, the glory, the victory, and the majesty. Everything in the heavens and on earth is yours, O LORD, and this is your kingdom. We adore you as the one who is over all things" (1 Chron. 29:11 NLT).

You will never exhaust his resources. At no time does he wave away your prayer with "Come back tomorrow. I'm tired, weary, depleted."

God is affluent! Wealthy in love, abundant in hope, overflowing in wisdom.

> No eye has seen, no ear has heard,
>   and no mind has imagined
> what God has prepared
>   for those who love him. (1 Cor. 2:9 NLT)

Your imagination is too timid to understand God's dream for you. He stands with you on the eastern side of the Jordan River, he gestures at the expanse of Canaan, and he tells you what he told Joshua: be strong and of good courage, for this is your inheritance (Josh. 1:6).

People of the Promise believe in the abundance of supernatural resources. Don't we need them? Are we not prone to depletions? How often do you find yourself thinking, *I'm out of solutions* or *There's no way this will work* or *I can't fix this?*

I recently spent the better part of an hour reciting the woes of my life to my wife. I felt overwhelmed by commitments and deadlines. I'd been sick with the flu. There was tension at the church between some coworkers. I'd just returned from an international trip, and jet lag was having its way with me. We'd received word of friends who were getting a divorce. And then, to top it off, I received a manuscript from my editors that was bloody with red ink. I actually looked for a chapter that didn't need a rewrite. There wasn't one. It was a train wreck.

If you could have read my mind, you would have thought you were perusing the textbook for Pessimism 101. *My work is in vain. I'm going to move to the Amazon jungle and live in a hut. I don't have what it takes to be a writer, minister, encourager . . . human being!*

After several minutes Denalyn interrupted me with a question. "Is God in this anywhere?" (I hate it when she does that.)

What had happened to me? I was focusing on my resources. I wasn't thinking about God. I wasn't consulting God. I wasn't turning to God. I wasn't talking about God. I'd limited my world to my strength, wisdom, and power. No wonder I was in a tailspin.

For such moments God gives this promise: "We are heirs—heirs of God and co-heirs with Christ" (Rom. 8:17).

The cronies of dismay, gloom, and dejection have no answer for the promise of inheritance. Tell them, "My Lord will help me. Strength is on the way. The gauge may be bouncing on Empty, but I will not run out of fuel. My Father will not allow it. I am a child of the living and loving God, and he will help me."

This resurrection life you received from God is not a timid, grave-tending life. It's adventurously expectant, greeting God with a childlike "What's next, Papa?" God's Spirit touches our spirits and confirms who we really are. We know who he is, and we know who we are: Father and children. And we know we are going to get what's coming to us—an unbelievable inheritance! (Rom. 8:15–17 THE MESSAGE)

To Timothy Gray we would have said, "Hey, Mr. Gray, you are a descendant of wealth, an heir to a fortune. Get out from under this bridge, and make your request."

To us the angels want to say:

"Hey, Lucado! Yeah, you with the rotten attitude. You are an heir to the joy of Christ. Why not ask Jesus to help you?"

"And you, Mr. Without-a-Clue. Aren't you an heir to God's storehouse of wisdom? Solicit some guidance, why don't you?"

"Mrs. Worrywart. Why do you let your fears steal your sleep? Jesus has abundant peace. Are you not a beneficiary of God's trust fund? Put in your request."

Understand your place in the family. You come to God not as a stranger but as an heir to the promise. You approach God's throne not as an interloper but as a child in whom the Spirit of God dwells.

One of the most famous stories in the Bible has to do with inheritance. The Hebrews had just been delivered from Egyptian captivity. God led them and Moses to the edge of the promised land and made this offer: "The LORD said to Moses, 'Send some men to explore the land of Canaan, which *I am giving* to the Israelites. From each ancestral tribe send one of its leaders'" (Num. 13:1–2, emphasis mine).

God did not tell the Israelites to conquer, take, invade, subject, or secure the land. He told them he was giving it to them. Their choice was clear: promises or circumstances? The circumstances said, "No way. Stay out. There are giants in the land." God's promise said, "The land is yours. The victory is yours. Take it."

All they had to do was trust his promise, despite the circumstances, and receive the gift. But they didn't. It was a bad decision with a forty-year probation penalty. God left them to wander in the wilderness for a generation, until a new breed of followers surfaced.

Joshua was the leader of that generation. Upon the death of Moses, God reissued the promised land offer. "After the death of Moses the servant of the LORD, the LORD said to Joshua son of Nun, Moses' aide: 'Moses my servant is dead. Now then, you and all these people, get ready to cross the Jordan River into the land I am about to give to them—to the Israelites. I will give you every place where you set your foot, as I promised Moses'" (Josh. 1:1–3).

We typically think of Joshua as taking the land. It's more precise to think of Joshua as taking God at his word. Joshua took the land, for sure. But he did so because he trusted God's promise. The great accomplishment of the Hebrew people was this: they lived out of their inheritance. In fact, the story ends with this declaration: "Then Joshua dismissed the people, each to their own inheritance" (Josh. 24:28).

Is that to say they had no challenges? The book of Joshua makes it clear that wasn't the case. The Jordan River was wide. The Jericho walls were high. The evil inhabitants of Canaan were not giving up without a fight. Still, Joshua led the Hebrews to cross the Jordan, bring down the walls of Jericho, and defeat the thirty-one enemy kings. Every time he faced a challenge, he did so with faith, because he trusted his inheritance.

What if you did the same?

Standing before you is a Jericho wall of fear. Brick upon brick of anxiety and dread. It's a stronghold that keeps you out of Canaan. Circumstances say, *Cower to your fears.* Your inheritance says otherwise: *You are a child of the King. His perfect love casts out fear. Move forward.*

Choose your inheritance.

Haunting you are the kings of confusion. Thanks to them, you've struggled with your identity and destiny. You've bought the lie that life has no absolutes or purpose. Then you remember your inheritance: Truth. Guidance from God. His Word to instruct you.

Choose your inheritance.

Is that to say all your challenges will disappear? They didn't for Joshua. He fought for seven years! But he knew more victory than defeat.

So can you. It comes down to a simple decision to believe and receive your position as an heir of God and coheir with Christ. "In this world we are like Jesus" (1 John 4:17). We aren't slaves or distant relatives. Our inheritance is every bit as abundant as that of Jesus himself. What he receives, we receive.

Suppose you are relaxing at home one evening when the doorbell rings. You answer the door to see a well-dressed man who introduces himself as an attorney who specializes in large estates.

"Might I come in and visit with you about a potential inheritance?"

Typically you wouldn't allow a stranger into your home. But did he say "inheritance"?

You offer him a seat at the table. He produces a document from his briefcase and begins with some questions. "Did your mother come from England?"

"Yes."

"Was her name Mary Jones?"

"Yes." Your pulse rate increases.

"Did she settle in Chicago? Work as a teacher? Marry John Smith and die five years ago in Florida?"

"Yes. Yes. Yes, and yes."

"And are you John Smith Jr.?"

"Yes!"

"Then we've been looking for you. Your mother inherited a large sum from her uncle. Now that inheritance is yours."

"It is?"

"Yes."

You think, *I can buy those new shoes at Dillard's.*

"It is quite sizable."

Maybe I should go to Nordstrom.

"Probably more than you could imagine."

Okay, Saks Fifth Avenue.

"You have inherited a gold mine in South Africa. It will take several years to work out all the inheritance, but in the meantime here is a down payment. Twenty million dollars."

Maybe I will buy Saks Fifth Avenue.

If this is the down payment, what is the entire inheritance going to be worth?

That, my friend, is the People of the Promise question. You are an heir with Christ of God's estate. He will provide what you need to face the challenges of life. He certainly did for Diet Eman.

Early in the morning hours of May 10, 1940, she awoke to what sounded like the beating of rugs. As the popping continued, the twenty-year-old Dutch girl climbed out of bed and scrambled with her parents to the front lawn. German planes buzzed through the sky and rained bullets upon The Hague. Hitler had assured the people of the Netherlands that he would respect their neutrality. That became yet another of his broken promises.

After getting back inside, the family turned on the radio and heard, "We are at war. German paratroopers have landed." Diet immediately thought about her boyfriend, Hein. The two had much in common. Both were raised in Christian homes, both were loyal to their homeland, and both were incensed at the German oppression of the Jews.

Not all Dutch believers were. Some advocated for a plan to avoid conflict and trust the will of God. But for Hein and Diet, the will of God was clear. Hein knew the *Mein Kampf* message. He told Diet, "[Hitler's] so full of hate, he's going to do something terrible!" By the end of 1941 the Nazis required Jews to wear yellow stars and banned them from travel. Many were receiving deportation notices to Germany.

Diet was contacted by a Jewish man who asked her for assistance. She and Hein knew that the risk to them was great. If they were caught, it could mean death. But they helped him anyway and arranged for him to go to Friesland to live with a farmer until the war was over.

What began as assistance to one man grew to a plan to help others. The stakes grew higher and higher. Hein spoke of contingency plans, of what to do if he was arrested. In one such conversation Diet sensed an inner voice saying, *You'd better have a good look at him.* Three days later, on April 26, 1944, he was arrested and carried off to prison.

Diet altered her appearance and identification. Her tactics were not enough. Within a few weeks she found herself in prison as well, where her only hope was the promises of God. One day she used a bobby pin and scratched the words of Jesus into the prison's brick wall: "Lo, I am with you always, even unto the end" (Matt. 28:20 KJV).

A few weeks later she, along with many other prisoners, was moved to a concentration camp. There were few rations and no soap, towels, or toilet paper. At times she wondered if she was losing her mind. When she was finally given a hearing, she rehearsed the story she would tell the Nazis, and she clung to two promises she remembered from Scripture: not a hair on her head would be touched (Luke 21:18), and she needn't fear when she appeared before the authorities (Matt. 10:19). She was allowed to go back to the barracks that day, and two weeks later she was freed.

Hein, however, was in Dachau. One of his fellow prisoners later told Diet that Hein displayed an inner beauty, that he loved life and loved Christ. He became weak at the end, so weak he could not work. He was removed from the barracks and never seen again.

She did receive one more message. Sometime before his death

Hein had scribbled a note on a piece of toilet paper, wrapped it in brown paper, addressed it, and thrown it from a window of a prisoner transport train. Someone found it and, amazingly, put it in the mail. The note read:

> Darling, don't count on our seeing each other again soon. . . . Here we see again that we do not decide our own lives. . . . Even if we won't see each other again on earth, we will never be sorry for what we did, that we took this stand. And know, Diet, that of every last human being in this world, I loved you most.[2]

In my mind's eye I envision young Diet lying in her bed, running her finger across the words she etched into the wall. The prisoners are hungry. Her stomach growls, and her body is weak. But she chooses to focus on this promise, this inheritance: *"Lo, I am with you always, even unto the end."*

I try to imagine the sight of Hein in Dachau. Men with skeletal frames roam about the prison yard. The scent of death is in the air, and Hein knows his time is short. In what must have been his final opportunity to write, he dips a pen in the inkwell of hope and scribbles, *"We will never be sorry for what we did."*

Where did this couple quarry such courage? Where did they find their hope? How did they avoid despair? Simple. They trusted God's great promises. What about you? What message are you carving on the wall? What words are you writing? Choose hope, not despair. Choose life, not death. Choose God's promises.

You don't have to sleep under the overpass anymore. You are a new person. Live like one.

It's time for you to live out of your inheritance.

CHAPTER 5

Your Prayers
Have Power

GOD'S PROMISE

When a believing person prays,
great things happen.

—James 5:16 NCV

I accompanied Denalyn on some errand running recently. We stopped at a store called OfficeMax so she could buy a calendar. As we walked through the parking lot, I pointed at the sign and said, "Honey, this is my store. Office*Max*!"

She was unimpressed.

I hurried to the front door and held it open.

"Come into *my* store."

She rolled her eyes. I used to think the rolling of the eyes was a gesture of frustration. After thirty-five years I now realize it is a symbol of admiration! After all, she does it so often.

I continued my posturing as we shopped, thanking her for coming to *my* store to buy products off *my* shelves. She just rolled her eyes at me. I think she was speechless.

When we reached the checkout line, I told the clerk my status. I arched an eyebrow and deepened my voice. "Hi, I'm Max."

She smiled and processed the sale.

"As in OfficeMax."

She looked at me and then at Denalyn, who rolled her eyes again. Such admiration for her husband. I was beginning to blush.

"I am the boss of this place," I told the clerk.

"Really?" She looked at me with no smile.

"Why don't you just take the afternoon off?"

"What?"

"Take the afternoon off. If people ask, tell them that Max of OfficeMax said you could go home."

This time she stopped and looked at me. "Sir, you've got the name, but you don't have the clout."

She was right about me, but the same cannot be said about you.

If you have taken on the name of Christ, you have clout with the most powerful being in the universe. When you speak, God listens. When you pray, heaven takes note. "When two of you get together on anything at all on earth and make a prayer of it, my Father in heaven goes into action" (Matt. 18:19 THE MESSAGE).

Your prayers impact the actions of God.

For proof, consider the story of Elijah. He lived eight centuries prior to the birth of Jesus. The Northern Kingdom had twenty kings, each one of whom was evil. The evilest of the monarchs was Ahab.

His life is described in this sad summary: "There was never anyone like Ahab, who sold himself to do evil in the eyes of the LORD, urged on by Jezebel his wife. He behaved in the vilest manner by going after idols, like the Amorites the LORD drove out before Israel" (1 Kings 21:25–26).

This was as dark a time as we ever read about in the history of Israel. The leaders were corrupt, and the hearts of the people were cold. But comets are most visible against a black sky. And in the midst of the darkness, a fiery comet by the name of Elijah appeared.

The name Elijah means "My God is Jehovah,"[1] and Elijah lived up to his name. He gave King Ahab an unsolicited weather report. "As the LORD, the God of Israel, lives, whom I serve, there will be neither dew nor rain in the next few years except at my word" (1 Kings 17:1).

Elijah's attack was calibrated. Baal was the fertility god of the pagans, the god to whom they looked for rain and fertile fields. Elijah called for a showdown: the true God of Israel against the false god of the pagans. How could Elijah be so confident of the impending drought? Because he had prayed.

Nine centuries later the prayers of Elijah were used as a model. "When a believing person prays, great things happen. Elijah was a human being just like us. He prayed that it would not rain, and it did not rain on the land for three and a half years! Then Elijah prayed again, and the rain came down from the sky, and the land produced crops again" (James 5:16–18 NCV).

James was impressed that a prayer of such power came from a person so common. "Elijah was a human being, even as we are" (James 5:17), but his prayers were heard because he prayed, not eloquently, but earnestly. This was not a casual prayer or a comfortable prayer but a radical prayer. "Do whatever it takes, Lord," Elijah begged, "even if that means no water."

"So Ahab sent word throughout all Israel and assembled the prophets on Mount Carmel. Elijah went before the people and said, 'How long will you waver between two opinions? If the LORD is God, follow him; but if Baal is God, follow him.' But the people said nothing" (1 Kings 18:20–21). Elijah put the 450 prophets of Baal and the Israelites in a decision posture: How long are you going to waver between two opinions? The word translated *waver* is the exact Hebrew word used later for "danced" (v. 26). How long are you going to do this dance? You dance with God and then Baal. How long will this continue?

What happens next is one of the greatest stories in the Bible. Elijah told the 450 prophets of Baal: "You take a bull; I'll take a bull. You build an altar; I'll build an altar. You ask your god to send fire; I'll ask my God to send fire. The God who answers by fire is the true God."

The prophets of Baal agreed and went first.

At noon Elijah began to taunt them. "Shout louder!" he said. "Surely he is a god! Perhaps he is deep in thought, or busy, or traveling. Maybe he is sleeping and must be awakened." (v. 27)

(Elijah would have flunked a course in diplomacy.) Though the prophets of Baal cut themselves and raved all afternoon, nothing happened. Finally Elijah asked for his turn. He poured four jugs of water (remember, this was a time of drought) over the altar three times. Then he prayed.

> LORD, the God of Abraham, Isaac and Israel, let it be known today that you are God in Israel and that I am your servant and have done all these things at your command. Answer me, LORD, answer me, so these people will know that you, LORD, are God, and that you are turning their hearts back again. (vv. 36–37)

Note how quickly God answered.

> Then the fire of the LORD fell and burned up the sacrifice, the wood, the stones and the soil, and also licked up the water in the trench.
> When all the people saw this, they fell prostrate and cried, "The LORD—he is God! The LORD—he is God!" (vv. 38–39)

No request for fire was made. Just the heart of the prophet was revealed, and *pow!* The altar was ablaze. God delighted in hearing Elijah's prayer. God delights in hearing yours as well.

But why? Why would our prayers matter? We can't even get the plumber to call us back, so why would God listen to our ideas?

Simple. Your prayers matter to God because you matter to God. You aren't just anybody; as we saw in the last chapter, you are his child.

I have a friend who owns a successful business. He employs more than five hundred people in a dozen states. He appreciates each and every one of them. Yet he treats three of his workers with partiality. They are his sons. While he hears all requests, he especially hears theirs. They are being trained to run the family business.

So are you. When God saved you, he enlisted you. He gave not only forgiveness for your past but also authority in the present and a role in the future.

This life is on-the-job training for eternity. God is preparing you to reign with him in heaven. "If we endure, we will also reign with him" (2 Tim. 2:12). We shall "reign on the earth" (Rev. 5:10). We are part of God's family. Ruling the universe is the family business. When the sons of my friend ask him, "Can we open a branch in Topeka?" or "Can we add a new product to our catalog?" or "What would you think if we brought on a new accountant?" the father listens. He has a vested interest in their development. Our Father has a vested interest in ours. When you, as God's child, seek to honor the family business, God hears your requests.

> "God, grant me deeper faith so I can serve you."
> "God, please grant my promotion so I can honor you."
> "God, show me where we can live and best bring glory to
>   your name."
> "God, please give me a spouse so I can serve you better."

God hears these prayers as quickly as they are offered. Why? Because they come from his child.

Will God do what you ask? Perhaps. Or perhaps he will do more than you imagined. He knows what is best. Stand firmly on this promise: "When a believing person prays, great things happen" (James 5:16 NCV). You are never without hope, because you are never without prayer.

A dramatic illustration of this promise is found among the Christians of Russia. For eight decades of the twentieth century, Christians in Russia experienced systemic persecution from the communist government. Schoolteachers would hold up a Bible and ask kindergarten students if they had seen such a book in their homes. If a student said yes, a government official would visit the family. Pastors and lay people were imprisoned, never to be heard from again. The government required pastors to visit their offices once a week to report on any new visitors. Pastors were required to present sermon topics for approval.

This was the world in which a man named Dmitri practiced his faith. He and his family lived in a small village four hours from Moscow. The nearest church was a three-day walk, making it impossible for them to attend church more than twice a year.

Dmitri began to teach his family Bible stories and verses. Neighbors got wind of the lessons and wanted to participate. When the group grew to twenty-five people, officials took notice and demanded he stop. He refused. When the group reached fifty people, Dmitri was dismissed from his factory job, his wife was fired from her teaching position, and his sons were expelled from school.

Still he continued. When the gathering increased to seventy-five people, there wasn't enough room in his house. Villagers squeezed into every available corner and closed in around the windows so they might listen to this man of God teach. One night a group of soldiers burst into the gathering. A soldier grabbed Dmitri and slapped him back and forth across the face. He then warned Dmitri to stop or something worse would happen to him.

As the officer turned to leave, a small grandmother stepped in his path and waved a finger in his face. "You have laid hands on a man of God and you will *not* survive!"

Within two days the officer was dead from a heart attack.

The fear of God spread, and one hundred fifty people showed up for the next house meeting. Dmitri was arrested and sentenced to seventeen years in prison.

His jail cell was so small that he needed only one step to reach each wall. He was the only believer among fifteen hundred prisoners. The officials tortured him, and the prisoners mocked him. But he never broke.

Each morning at daybreak Dmitri stood by his bed, faced eastward, raised his arms to God, and sang a song of praise. Other prisoners would jeer. Still he sang.

Whenever he found a scrap of paper, he scribbled down a verse or story from memory. When the paper was completely filled, he took it to the corner of his cell and affixed it to a damp pillar as a sacrifice to Jesus. Officials routinely spotted the papers, removed them, and beat Dmitri. Still he worshipped.

This went on for seventeen years. On only one occasion did he nearly recant his faith. Guards convinced him that his wife had been murdered and his children were wards of the state.

The thought was more than Dmitri could bear. He agreed to renounce his faith in Christ. The guards told him they would return the next day with a document. All he had to do was sign it, and he would be released.

The officials were sure of their victory. What they did not know was this: when believing people pray, great things happen.

Believing people were praying for Dmitri. A thousand kilometers away, that night his family sensed a special burden to pray for him. They knelt in a circle and interceded passionately for his protection. Miraculously, the Lord allowed Dmitri to hear the voices of his loved ones as they prayed. He knew they were safe.

The next morning when the guards came for his signature, they saw a renewed man. His face was calm, and his eyes were resolute. "I am not signing anything!" he told them. "In the night, God let me hear the voices of my wife and my children and my brother praying for me. You lied to me! I now know that my wife is alive and physically well. I know that my sons are with her. I also know that they are all still in Christ. So I am not signing anything!"

The officials beat him and threatened to execute him, but Dmitri's resolve only increased. He still worshipped in the mornings and posted verses on the pillar. Finally the authorities had all they could take. They dragged Dmitri from his cell through the corridor in the center of the prison toward the place of execution. As they did, fifteen hundred criminals raised their hands and began to sing the song of praise they had heard Dmitri sing each morning.

The jailers released their hold on him and stepped back. "Who are you?"

"I am a son of the Living God, and Jesus is His name!" Dmitri was taken back to his cell. Sometime later he was released and returned to his family.[2]

You'll likely never find yourself in a Russian prison, but you may find yourself in an impossible situation. You'll feel outnumbered and outmaneuvered. You'll want to quit. Could I ask you, implore you, to memorize this promise and ask God to bring it to mind on that day? Write it where you will find it. Tattoo it, if not on your skin at least on your heart: "When a believing person prays, great things happen" (James 5:16 NCV).

Prayer is not the last resort; it is the first step. God has power you've never seen, strength you've never known. He delighted in and answered Elijah's prayer. God delighted in and answered the prayers of Dmitri and his family. God delights in and will answer ours as well.

Now if you'll excuse me, I have some business to attend to. I need to check on RE/MAX, CarMax, and Lotto Max. It's not easy keeping up with all these businesses.

CHAPTER 6

Grace for the Humble

GOD'S PROMISE

God resists the proud,
But gives grace to the humble.

—1 Peter 5:5 NKJV

When he wasn't flying his private jet across the Atlantic or watching sunsets from the deck of one of his yachts, he was living a life of luxury inside his ten-thousand-square-foot Lexington Avenue penthouse in New York City.

His yacht *Bull* cost seven million dollars. His jet cost twenty-four million. He had a home in France, a beach home in Montauk, and a house in Palm Beach. He had boats and cars. His wife had furs and designer handbags, Wedgewood china, and Christofle silver. When it came to decor, she spared no expense. Gold sconces lined the wallpaper. Central Asian rugs covered the floors. Greek and Egyptian statues competed for the approval of guests.

Everyone wanted to know him. People stood in line to shake his hand. People like Steven Spielberg and Elie Wiesel. To stand in his Manhattan office was to stand in the epicenter of investment success.

Or so it seemed until the morning of December 10, 2008. That's when the charade ended. That's when Bernie Madoff, this generation's most infamous scam artist, sat down with his wife and two sons and confessed that it was a "giant Ponzi scheme . . . just one big lie."[1]

Over the next days, weeks, and months, the staggering details became public knowledge. Madoff had masterminded a twenty-year-long shell game, the largest financial crime in US history. He had swindled people out of billions of dollars.

His collapse was of biblical proportions. In short order he was stripped of everything. No money. No future. No family. One of his sons committed suicide. His wife went into seclusion. And seventy-one-year-old Bernie Madoff was sentenced to spend the rest of his life as prisoner number 61727-054 in the Federal Correction Complex of Butner, North Carolina.

Why did he do it? What makes a man live a lie for decades? What was the trade-off for Madoff?

In a word, status. According to one biographer:

> As a kid, he was spurned and humiliated for what was perceived to be his inferior intellect. . . . He was rejected by one girl after another . . . relegated to lesser classes and lesser schools. . . .
>
> But he excelled at making money, and with it came the stature that once had eluded him.[2]

Stature. Madoff was addicted to adulation. He was hooked on recognition. He wanted the applause of people, and money was his way of earning it. He elbowed and clawed his way to the top of the mountain, only to discover that its peak is slippery and crowded. If only he had known this promise: "God resists the proud, but gives grace to the humble" (1 Peter 5:5 NKJV).

His story exemplifies the passage, but if you want to see an even more dramatic picture of the downfall of pride, open your Bible to the book of Daniel, and read the story of Nebuchadnezzar. The money and descent of Madoff was small potatoes compared to the vast possessions and sudden free fall of the king of ancient Babylon.

He overthrew Jerusalem in 605 BC. Among his Hebrew captives were four young men, Daniel, Shadrach, Meshach, and Abednego. After some years he built a ninety-foot-tall golden statue in his honor and commanded the people to bow down before it. Shadrach, Meshach, and Abednego refused. So the king heated the furnace to seven times its normal temperature and threw them into the fire. When they came out unsinged, he was amazed. But did King Nebuchadnezzar humble himself?

Sadly, no.

Years passed. Nebuchadnezzar was enjoying a time of peace and prosperity. His enemies were held at bay. His wealth was secure. Yet in the midst of all this, he had a dream. His fortune-tellers could not explain it. But Daniel could. Nebuchadnezzar described the dream:

> I looked, and there before me stood a tree in the middle of the land. Its height was enormous. The tree grew large and strong and its top touched the sky; it was visible to the ends of the earth. Its leaves were beautiful, its fruit abundant, and on it was food for all. Under it the wild animals found shelter, and the birds lived in its branches; from it every creature was fed. (Dan. 4:10–12)

Nebuchadnezzar went on to describe how the tree was cut down by a messenger from heaven. Its branches were trimmed and fruit scattered. Only a stump remained. The voice from heaven then made a pronouncement:

> Let him be drenched with the dew of heaven, and let him live with the animals among the plants of the earth. Let his mind be changed from that of a man and let him be given the mind of an animal, till seven times pass by for him. (vv. 15–16)

Daniel listened to the dream and gulped. He was astonished and troubled by what he heard.

At this point in history Nebuchadnezzar had no peers. He was the uncontested ruler of the world. Babylon rose out of the desert plains like a Manhattan skyline. The Hanging Gardens of Babylon, which he built for his wife, were one of the Seven Wonders of the Ancient World. The walls of his royal palace were 320 feet high and 80 feet thick. Two four-horse chariots could ride abreast on them.[3] The mighty

Euphrates River flowed through the city. During Nebuchadnezzar's forty-three-year rule, greater Babylon's population reached as high as half a million people.[4] The king was part oil baron, part royalty, part hedge-fund billionaire. Were he alive today, he would dominate the *Forbes* list of billionaires.

But all of this was about to end.

Daniel told him:

> Your Majesty, you are that tree! . . .
>
> . . . You will be driven away from people and will live with the wild animals; you will eat grass like the ox and be drenched with the dew of heaven. Seven times will pass by for you until you acknowledge that the Most High is sovereign over all kingdoms on earth and gives them to anyone he wishes. The command to leave the stump of the tree with its roots means that your kingdom will be restored to you when you acknowledge that Heaven rules. (vv. 22, 25–26)

Nebuchadnezzar thought he was in charge. He believed he ran his world, perhaps the whole world.

Daniel urged him to repent.

> Therefore, Your Majesty, be pleased to accept my advice: Renounce your sins by doing what is right, and your wickedness by being kind to the oppressed. It may be that then your prosperity will continue. (v. 27)

But did Nebuchadnezzar change?

> Twelve months later, as the king was walking on the roof of the royal palace of Babylon, he said, "Is not this the great Babylon I have built as the royal residence, by my mighty power and for the glory of my majesty?" (vv. 29–30)

God gave the king another year to climb down from his pomp-ous throne. But he never did. Oh, the proliferation of pronouns. "I have built," "my mighty power," "my majesty." The king was all about the king.

God had sent him at least three messages. The message of the fiery furnace: *Jehovah God is greater than fire.* The message of the dream: *Today's massive tree is tomorrow's ugly stump.* The warning of Daniel: *Humble yourself before it is too late.*

Nebuchadnezzar refused to listen.

Even as the words were on his lips, a voice came from heaven, "This is what is decreed for you, King Nebuchadnezzar: Your royal authority has been taken from you. You will be driven away from people and will live with the wild animals; you will eat grass like the ox." (vv. 31–32)

The king became an ancient version of Howard Hughes: cork-screw fingernails, wild hair, animalistic.

He was driven away from people and ate grass like the ox. His body was drenched with the dew of heaven until his hair grew like the feathers of an eagle and his nails like the claws of a bird. (v. 33)

When the mighty fall, the fall is mighty. One minute he was on the cover of *Time* magazine; the next he was banished like a caged creature. And we are left with a lesson: God hates pride.

Do you see a person wise in their own eyes?
There is more hope for a fool than for them. (Prov. 26:12)

Woe to those who are wise in their own eyes
and clever in their own sight. (Isa. 5:21)

The LORD detests all the proud of heart. (Prov. 16:5)

> I hate pride and arrogance,
>   evil behavior and perverse speech. (Prov. 8:13)

When pride comes, then comes disgrace. (Prov. 11:2)

Why the strong language? Why the blanket condemnation? How do we explain God's abhorrence of the haughty heart?

Simple. God resists the proud because the proud resist God. Arrogance stiffens the knee so it will not kneel, hardens the heart so it will not admit to sin. The heart of pride never confesses, never repents, never asks for forgiveness. Indeed, the arrogant never feel the need for forgiveness. Pride is the hidden reef that shipwrecks the soul.

Pride not only prevents reconciliation with God; it prevents reconciliation with people. How many marriages have collapsed beneath the weight of foolish pride? How many apologies have gone unoffered due to the lack of humility? How many wars have sprouted from the rocky soil of arrogance?

Pride comes at a high price. Don't pay it. Choose instead to stand on the offer of grace. "God resists the proud, but gives grace to the humble" (1 Peter 5:5 NKJV). To the degree God hates arrogance, he loves humility. Isn't it easy to see why? Humility is happy to do what pride will not. The humble heart is quick to acknowledge the need for God, eager to confess sin, willing to kneel before heaven's mighty hand.

God has a special place for the humble of heart.

> Though the LORD is supreme,
>   he takes care of those who are humble,
>   but he stays away from the proud. (Ps. 138:6 NCV)

The high and lofty one who lives in eternity,
    the Holy One, says this:
"I live in the high and holy place
    with those whose spirits are contrite and humble.
I restore the crushed spirit of the humble
    and revive the courage of those with repentant hearts."
    (Isa. 57:15 NLT)

Wonderful freedom is found in the forest of humility. I experienced it sometime back as I sat in a circle. There were twenty of us in all. A beautician sat to my right. A lawyer to my left. One fellow wore tattoos, another a gray flannel suit. One arrived on a Harley. A couple showed up late. More than one of us arrived in a grumpy mood. All ages. Both sexes. Several races. We were an assorted lot. With one exception we had nothing in common.

But that one exception was significant. We were confessed lawbreakers. Wrongdoers every one of us. Each person in the room had received a piece of paper from a uniformed officer. So there we sat in a Defensive Driving class.

I'd dreaded the day all week. Who wants to share a Saturday with a roomful of strangers reviewing the Texas Driver Handbook? But I was surprised. After a short time we felt like friends. The bonding began with the introductions. Around the circle we went, giving our names and confessions.

"I'm Max. I went forty-five miles per hour in a thirty-mile-per-hour zone."

"I'm Sue. I made an illegal U-turn."

"Hello, I'm Bob. Got caught passing in a no-passing zone."

As each one spoke, the rest nodded, moaned, and dabbed tears. We felt one another's pain.

No masks. No make-believe. No games or excuses. Costumes

checked at the door. Pretense left at home. Charades and shams were unnecessary. Might as well admit our failures and enjoy the day. So we did, and the humility created relief. This was God's plan all along.

God gives grace to the humble because the humble are hungry for grace.

I'm wondering if you'd be willing to join me in a prayer of repentance, repentance from arrogance. What have we done that God didn't first do? What do we have that God didn't first give us? Have any of us ever built anything that God can't destroy? Have we created any monument that the Master of the stars can't reduce to dust?

> "To whom will you compare me?
>> Or who is my equal?" says the Holy One.
> Lift up your eyes and look to the heavens:
>> Who created all these?
> He who brings out the starry host one by one
>> and calls forth each of them by name.
> Because of his great power and mighty strength,
>> not one of them is missing. (Isa. 40:25–26)

I like the joke about the arrogant man who took God's preeminence to task. He looked up into the heavens and declared, "I can do what you can do! I can create a person out of dust! I understand the systems of life and science!"

God accepted the offer. "All right," he told the buffoon. "Let's see what you can do."

The man reached down and took a handful of dirt. But before the man could go further, God interrupted him. "I thought you said you could do what I did."

"I can."

"Then," God instructed, "get your own dirt."

Humility is healthy because humility is honest.

Sometime ago I partnered with musician Michael W. Smith for a ministry weekend in Asheville, North Carolina. The retreat was held at The Cove, a beautiful facility that is owned and maintained by the Billy Graham Evangelistic Association.

A few hours before the event, Michael and I met to go over the weekend schedule. But Michael was so moved by what he had just experienced that he hardly discussed the retreat. Michael had just met with Billy Graham. The famous evangelist was, at the time, ninety-four years old. His thoughts turned to what might be said about him at his funeral. He told Michael that he hoped his name would not be mentioned.

"What?" Michael asked.

"I hope only that the name of the Lord Jesus be lifted up."

Billy Graham has preached to 215 million people in person and hundreds of millions of others through media. He has filled stadiums on every continent. He has advised every US president from Truman to Obama. He has consistently been near the top of every most-admired list. Yet he doesn't want to be mentioned at his own funeral.

Can it be that when we realize God is so big, we finally see how small we are?

Those who walk in pride God is able to humble. But those who walk in humility God is able to use.

King Nebuchadnezzar learned this lesson. It took seven years, but he got the point.

At the end of that time, I, Nebuchadnezzar, raised my eyes toward heaven, and my sanity was restored. Then I praised the Most High; I honored and glorified him who lives forever. . . .

. . . Now I, Nebuchadnezzar, praise and exalt and glorify the King of heaven, because everything he does is right and all his ways are just. And those who walk in pride he is able to humble. (Dan. 4:34, 37)

You might want to underline that last sentence. *Those who walk in pride God is able to humble.* It's better to humble yourself than to wait for God to do it for you.

CHAPTER 7

God Gets You

GOD'S PROMISE

Our high priest is able to
understand our weaknesses.

—Hebrews 4:15 NCV

On a splendid April afternoon in 2008, two college women's softball teams—one from Oregon, one from Washington—squared off beneath the blue sky of the Cascade Mountains. Inside a chain-link fence before a hundred fans, the two teams played a decisive game. The winner would advance to the division playoffs. The loser would hang up the gloves and go home.

The Western Oregon Wolves were a sturdy team that boasted several strong batters, but Sara Tucholsky was not one of them. She hit .153 and played in the game only because the first-string right fielder had muffed a play earlier in the day. Sara had never hit a home run, but on that Saturday, with two runners on base, she connected with a curveball and sent it sailing over the left-field fence.

In her excitement Sara missed first base. Her coach shouted for her to return and touch it. When she turned and started back, something popped in her knee, and down she went. She dragged herself back to the bag, pulled her knee to her chest in pain, and asked the first-base coach, "What do I do?"

The umpire wasn't sure. He knew if any of Sara's teammates assisted her, she would be out. Sara knew if she tried to stand, she would collapse. Her team couldn't help her. Her leg couldn't support her. How could she cross home plate? The umpires huddled to talk.[1]

And while they huddle and Sara groans, may I make a comparison? Blame it on the preacher in me, but I see an illustration in this moment. You and I have a lot in common with Sara Tucholsky. We, too, have stumbled. Not in baseball, but in life. In morality, honesty, integrity. We have done our best, only to trip and fall. Our finest efforts have left us flat on our backs. Like Sara, we are weakened, not with torn ligaments, but with broken hearts, weary spirits, and fading vision. The distance between where we are and where we want to be is impassable. What do we do? Where do we turn?

I suggest we turn to one of the sweetest promises:

> For our high priest [Jesus] is able to understand our weaknesses. He was tempted in every way that we are, but he did not sin. Let us, then, feel very sure that we can come before God's throne where there is grace. There we can receive mercy and grace to help us when we need it. (Heb. 4:15–16 NCV)

We have a high priest who is able to understand. Since he understands, we find mercy and grace when we need it. We are not left to languish. When we fall, we are not forgotten. When we stumble, we aren't abandoned. Our God gets us.

Theology textbooks discuss this promise under the heading "Incarnation." The stunning idea is simply this: God, for a time, became one of us. "The Word became flesh and made his dwelling among us. We have seen his glory, the glory of the one and only Son, who came from the Father, full of grace and truth" (John 1:14).

God became flesh in the form of Jesus Christ. He was miraculously conceived, yet naturally delivered. He was born, yet born of a virgin.

Had Jesus simply descended to earth in the form of a mighty being, we would respect him but never would draw near to him. After all, how could God understand what it means to be human?

Had Jesus been biologically conceived with two earthly parents, we would draw near to him, but would we want to worship him? After all, he would be no different than you and me.

But if Jesus was both—God and man at the same time—then we

have the best of both worlds. Neither his humanity nor deity compromised. He was fully human. He was fully divine. Because of the first, we draw near. Because of the latter, we worship.

Such is the message of Colossians 1:15–16.

> The Son is the image of the invisible God, the firstborn over all creation. For in him all things were created: things in heaven and on earth, visible and invisible, whether thrones or powers or rulers or authorities; all things have been created through him and for him.

Not one drop of divinity was lost in the change to humanity. Though Jesus appeared human, he was actually God. The fullness of God, every bit of him, took residence in the body of Christ. "It was the Father's good pleasure for all the fullness to dwell in Him" (Col. 1:19 NASB). The star maker, for a time, built cabinets in Nazareth.

Jesus may have looked human, but those nearest him knew he was prone to divine exclamations. Every so often Jesus let his divinity take over. The bystanders had no option but to step back and ask, "What kind of man is this? Even the winds and the waves obey him!" (Matt. 8:27).

Some years ago I served as the teacher at a weeklong Bible retreat. There is much to recall about the event. The food was phenomenal. The seaside setting was spectacular. I made several new friends. Yet, of all the memories, the one I will never forget is the Friday night basketball game.

The idea was hatched the moment David arrived. The attendees did not know he was coming, but as soon as he walked into the room, they knew who he was: David Robinson. NBA All-Star. MVP. Three-time Olympian. Two-time gold medal winner. Dream Team member. Two-time NBA champion. College All-American. Seven feet and one inch of raw talent. Body, ripped. Skills, honed. Basketball IQ, legendary.

By the end of the first day, someone asked me, "Any chance he would play basketball with us?" "Us" was a collection of pudgy, middle-aged, well-meaning but out-of-shape fellows. Bodies, plump. Skills, pathetic. Basketball IQ, slightly less than that of a squirrel.

Still, I asked David. And David, in an utter display of indulgence, said yes.

We scheduled the game, *the game*, for Friday night, the last night of the seminar. Attendance in the Bible classes declined. Attendance on the basketball court increased. Fellows who hadn't dribbled a ball since middle school could be seen heaving shot after shot at the basket. The net was seldom threatened.

The night of the game, *the game*, David walked onto the court for the first time all week. As he warmed up, the rest of us stopped. The ball fit in his hand like a tennis ball would in mine. He carried on conversations while dribbling the ball, spinning the ball on a finger, and passing the ball behind his back. When the game began, it was David and we children. He held back. We could tell. Even so, he still took one stride for our two. He caught the ball with one hand instead of two. When he threw the ball, it was more a missile than a pass. He played basketball at a level we could only dream about.

At one point—just for the fun of it, I suppose—he let loose. The same guy who had slam-dunked basketballs over Michael Jordan and Charles Barkley let it go. I suppose he just couldn't hold it back any longer. With three strides he roared from half court to the rim. The pudgy, middle-aged opposition cleared a path as he sailed, head level with the basket, and slammed the ball with a force that left the backboard shaking.

We gulped.

David smiled.

We got the message. That's how the game is meant to be played. We may have shared the same court, but we didn't share the same power.

I'm thinking the followers of Jesus might have had a similar thought. On the day Jesus commanded the demons to leave the possessed man and they did. On the day Jesus told the storm to be quiet and it was. On the days Jesus told the dead man to rise up, the dead daughter to sit up, the entombed Lazarus to come out, and he did, she did, and he did.

"God was pleased for all of himself to live in Christ" (Col. 1:19 NCV). Jesus was undiluted deity.

No wonder no one argued when he declared, "All authority in heaven and on earth has been given to me" (Matt. 28:18).

You think the moon affects the tides? It does. But Christ runs the moon. You think the United States is a superpower? The United States has only the power Christ gives and nothing more. He has authority over everything. And he has had it forever.

Yet, in spite of this lofty position, Jesus was willing for a time to forgo the privileges of divinity and enter humanity.

He was born just as all babies are born. His childhood was a common one. "Jesus grew in wisdom and stature, and in favor with God and man" (Luke 2:52). His body developed. His muscles strengthened. His bones matured. There is no evidence or suggestion that he was spared the inconveniences of adolescence. He may have been gangly or homely. He knew the pain of sore muscles and the sting of salt in an open wound. As an adult he was weary enough to sit down at a well (John 4:6) and sleepy enough to doze off in a rocking boat (Mark 4:35–38). He became hungry in the wilderness and thirsty on the cross. When the soldiers pounded the nails through his skin, a thousand nerve endings cried for relief. As he hung limp on the cross, two human lungs begged for oxygen.

The Word became flesh.

Does this promise matter? If you ever wonder if God understands you, it does. If you ever wonder if God listens, it does. If you ever wonder if the Uncreated Creator can, in a million years, compre-hend the challenges you face, then ponder long and hard the promise of the incarnation. Jesus is "able to understand our weaknesses" (Heb. 4:15 NCV). The One who hears your prayers understands your pain. He never shrugs or scoffs or dismisses physical struggle. He had a human body.

> Are you troubled in spirit? He was too. (John 12:27)
> Are you so anxious you could die? He was too. (Matt. 26:38)
> Are you overwhelmed with grief? He was too. (John 11:35)
> Have you ever prayed with loud cries and tears? He did too.
>   (Heb. 5:7)

He gets you.

So human he could touch his people. So mighty he could heal them. So human he spoke with an accent. So heavenly he spoke with authority. So human he could blend in unnoticed for thirty years. So mighty he could change history and be unforgotten for two thousand years. All man. Yet all God.

I once waded into the Jordan River. On a trip to Israel my fam-ily and I stopped to see the traditional spot of Jesus' baptism. It's a charming place. Sycamores cast their shadows. Birds chirp. The water invites. So I accepted the invitation and waded in to be baptized.

No one wanted to join me, so I immersed myself. I declared my belief in Christ and sank so low in the water I could touch the river bottom. When I did, I felt a stick and pulled it out. A baptism memento! Some people get certificates or Bibles; I like my stick. It's about as thick as your wrist, long as your forearm, and smooth as a baby's behind. I keep it on my office credenza so I can show it to fear-filled people.

When they chronicle their anxieties about the economy or their concerns about their kids, I hand them the stick. I tell them how God muddied his feet in our world of diapers, death, digestion, and disease. How John the Baptist told him to stay on the riverbank but Jesus wouldn't listen. How he came to earth for this very purpose—to become one of us. "Why, he might have touched this very stick," I like to say.

As they smile, I ask, "Since he came this far to reach us, can't we take our fears to him?" Read the promise again, slowly, thoughtfully.

> For our high priest [Jesus] is able to understand our weaknesses. He was tempted in every way that we are, but he did not sin. Let us, then, feel very sure that we can come before God's throne where there is grace. There we can receive mercy and grace to help us when we need it. (Heb. 4:15–16 NCV)

Some have pointed to the sinlessness of Jesus as evidence that he cannot fully understand us. If he never sinned, they reason, how could he understand the full force of sin? Simple. He felt it more than we do. We give in! He never did. We surrender. He never did. He stood before the tsunami of temptation and never wavered. In that manner he understands it more than anyone who ever lived.

And then, in his grandest deed, he volunteered to feel the consequences of sin. "God made him who had no sin to be sin for us, so that in him we might become the righteousness of God" (2 Cor. 5:21).

Jesus didn't deserve to feel the shame, but he felt it. He didn't deserve the humiliation, but he experienced it. He had never sinned, yet he was treated like a sinner. He became sin. All the guilt, remorse, and embarrassment—Jesus understands it.

Does this promise matter? To the hypocrite, it does. To the person with the hangover and fuzzy memory about last night's party, it does. To the cheater, slanderer, gossip, or scoundrel who comes to God with a humble spirit, it matters. It matters because they need to know that we can "approach God's throne of grace with confidence, so that we may receive mercy and find grace to help us in our time of need" (Heb. 4:16).

Because Jesus is human, he understands you.

Because he is divine, he can help you.

He is uniquely positioned to carry us home. Jesus does for us what Mallory Holtman did for Sara Tucholsky. Sara, remember, is the girl who tore an ACL during her home-run trot. When we left her, she was lying on the ground, clutching her knee with one hand and touching first base with the other. The umpires huddled. The players stood and watched. The fans shouted for someone to take Sara off the field, but she didn't want to leave. She wanted to cross home plate.

Mallory Holtman came up with a solution.

She played first base for the opposing team, Central Washington University. She was a senior and wanted a victory. A loss would end her season. You'd think Mallory would be happy to see the home run nullified. She wasn't.

"Hey," she said to the umpires. "Can I help her around the bases?"

"Why would you want to do that?" one asked. Before she could answer, the ump shrugged and said, "Do it."

So Mallory did. She signaled for the shortstop to help her, and the two walked toward the injured player. "We're going to pick you up and carry you around the bases."

By this time tears streaked Sara's cheeks. "Thank you."

Mallory and her friend put one hand under Sara's legs and the other hand under Sara's arms. The mission of mercy began. They paused long enough at second and third base to lower Sara's foot to touch the bases. By the time they headed home, the spectators had risen to their feet, Sara's teammates had gathered at home plate, and Sara was smiling like a homecoming queen.[2]

Well she should. The only one who could help did help. And because she did, Sara made it home.

God offers to do the same for you and me. Mallory's message for Sara is God's message for us: "I'm going to pick you up and carry you home." Let him, won't you? You cannot make it on your own. But Jesus has the strength you do not have. He is, after all, your high priest, able and willing to help in your time of need.

Let him do what he came to do. Let him carry you home.

CHAPTER 8

Christ Is Praying for You

GOD'S PROMISE

Jesus . . . is at the right hand of God
and is also interceding for us.

—Romans 8:34

We might assume the storms would have stopped. Jesus was on the earth, after all. He made the planet. He invented storm systems. He created the whole idea of atmosphere, wind, and rain. We might assume, for the time he was on his earth, that the world would have been storm-free, that God would have suspended the laws of nature and spared his Son the discomfort of slashing rains and howling winds.

Or at the very least we might suppose that Jesus would have walked around in a bubble. Like the one the pope uses when he drives through the crowds. Encircle our Savior with a protective shield so he doesn't get soaked, cold, afraid, or windswept. Jesus should be spared the storms of life.

And so should we. Lingering among the unspoken expectations of the Christian heart is this: *Now that I belong to God, I get a pass on the tribulations of life. I get a bubble. Others face storms. I live to help them. But face my own? No way.*

To follow Jesus is to live a storm-free life, right?

That expectation crashes quickly on the rocks of reality. The truth of the matter is this: life comes with storms. Jesus assures us, "In this world you will have trouble" (John 16:33). Storms will come to you, to me. They even came to Jesus' first disciples. "Immediately Jesus made the disciples get into the boat and go on ahead of him to the other side, while he dismissed the crowd. . . . Later that night . . . the boat was already a considerable distance from land, buffeted by the waves because the wind was against it" (Matt. 14:22–24).

Sometimes we create our own storms. We drink too much liquor or borrow too much money or hang out with the wrong crowd. We find ourselves in a storm of our own making.

This wasn't the case with the disciples. They were on the storm-tossed sea because Christ told them to be there. "Jesus made the disciples get into the boat." This wasn't Jonah seeking to escape God; these were disciples seeking to obey Jesus. These are missionaries who move overseas, only to have their support evaporate. These are business leaders who take the high road, only to see their efforts outbid by dishonest competitors. This is the couple who honors God in marriage, only to have an empty crib. This is the student who prepares, only to fall short on the exam. These are disciples who launch a boat as Jesus instructed, only to sail headfirst into a tempest. Storms come to the obedient.

And they come with a punch. "The boat was already a considerable distance from land, buffeted by the waves because the wind was against it" (v. 24).

Cool air surrounding the mountains east of the sea mixes with the warm tropical air near the water. The result is a tempest. Storms can be fierce on the Sea of Galilee.

Jesus dismissed the disciples at the evening hour. "When they had rowed about three or four miles" (John 6:19), the storm hit. Evening became night, night became windy and rainy, and before long their boat was riding the raging roller coaster of the Galilean sea. The five-mile trip should've taken not much more than an hour, but by the fourth watch (three o'clock to six o'clock in the morning) the disciples were still far from the shore.

They deserve credit. They did not turn around and go back to the shore; they persisted in obedience. They kept digging the oars into the water and pulling the craft across the sea. But they fought a losing battle. The storm left them too far from the shore, too long in the struggle, and too small in the waves.

Let's climb into the boat with them. Look at their rain-splattered faces. What do you see? Fear, for sure. Doubt? Absolutely. You may even hear a question shouted over the wind. "Anyone know where Jesus is?"

The question is not recorded in the text, but it was surely asked. It is today. When a ferocious storm pounces on obedient disciples, where in the world is Jesus?

The answer is clear and surprising: praying.

Jesus had gone "up on a mountainside by himself to pray" (Matt. 14:23). There is no indication that he did anything else. He didn't eat. He didn't chat. He didn't sleep. He prayed. Jesus was so intent in prayer that he persisted even though his robe was soaked and his hair was matted. After he'd served all day, he prayed all night. He felt the gale-force winds and the skin-stinging rain. He, too, was in the storm, but still he prayed.

Or should we say he was in the storm, *so* he prayed? Was the storm the reason for his intercession? Do his actions here describe his first course of action: to pray for his followers? During storms he is "at the right hand of God and is also interceding for us" (Rom. 8:34).

The Greek word in this verse that is translated "interceding" is a stout verb. It carries the sense of making specific requests or petitions before someone.[1] Festus, governor of Judea, used the Greek word for *intercede* when he spoke to the king about the apostle Paul. "King Agrippa, and all who are present with us, you see this man! The whole Jewish community has petitioned me about him in Jerusalem and here in Caesarea, shouting that he ought not to live any longer" (Acts 25:24).

Biblically speaking, this is what intercessors do. They bring passionate and specific requests before God.

Ponder this promise: Jesus, right now, at this moment, in the midst of your storm, is interceding for you. The King of the universe is speaking on your behalf. He is calling out to the heavenly Father. He is urging the help of the Holy Spirit. He is advocating for a special blessing to be sent your way. You do not fight the wind and waves alone. It's not up to you to find a solution. You have the mightiest Prince and the holiest Advocate standing up for you. When Stephen was about to be martyred for his faith, he "gazed steadily into heaven and saw the glory of God, and he saw Jesus standing in the place of honor at God's right hand" (Acts 7:55 NLT).

Jesus stood up for Stephen.

Ever had anyone stand up for you? The answer is yes. Jesus stands at this very moment, offering intercession on your behalf.

"Grant Mary the strength to face this interview!"
"Issue to Tom the wisdom necessary to be a good father!"
"Defeat the devil, who seeks to rob Allison of her sleep!"

"Where is Jesus?" Peter and crew may have asked.
"Where is Jesus?" the bedridden, the enfeebled, the
    impoverished, the overstressed, the isolated ask.

Where is he? He is in the presence of God, praying for us.

He says to you what he said to Peter. Knowing the apostle was about to be severely tested by Satan, Jesus assured him, "But I have prayed for you, that your faith should not fail" (Luke 22:32 NKJV).

Jesus prayed for Peter. He stood up for Stephen. He promises to pray and stand up for you. "Therefore he is able to save completely those who come to God through him, because he always lives to intercede for them" (Heb. 7:25).

When we forget to pray, he remembers to pray.
When we are full of doubt, he is full of faith.
Where we are unworthy to be heard, he is ever worthy to be
    heard.

———

Jesus is the sinless and perfect high priest. When he speaks, all of heaven listens.

Unshakable hope is the firstborn offspring of this promise. We'd like to know the future, but we don't. We long to see the road ahead, but we can't. We'd prefer to have every question answered, but Jesus has, instead, chosen to tell us this much: "I will pray you through the storm."

Are the prayers of Jesus answered? Of course.

Will you make it through this storm? I think you know the answer.

A person might object. If Jesus was praying, why did the storm even happen? Wouldn't an interceding Jesus guarantee a storm-free life? My answer: absolutely! That storm-free life will be inaugurated in the eternal kingdom. Between now and then, since this is a fallen world and since the devil still stirs doubt and fear, we can count on storms. But we can also count on the presence and prayers of Christ in the midst of them.

My friend Chris experienced a storm when he was nine years old. He was diagnosed with a case of mononucleosis. The doctor ordered him to stay indoors for the entire summer. Chris was a rambunctious, athletic, outgoing kid. To be told to spend a summer indoors? No Little League baseball, fishing trips, or bike rides? Might as well trap an eagle in a birdcage.

This was a nine-year-old's version of a tempest.

Chris's dad, however, was a man of faith. He resolved to find something good in the quarantine. He sold guitars in his drugstore and wasn't a half-bad guitarist himself. So he gave Chris a guitar. Each morning he taught his son a new chord or technique and told him to practice it all day. Chris did. Turns out, he had a knack for playing the guitar. By the end of the summer, Chris was playing Willie Nelson tunes and beginning to write some songs of his own.

Within a few years he was leading worship in churches. Within a few decades he was regarded as the "most sung songwriter in the world."[2] Perhaps you've heard some of his music: "How Great Is Our God," "Holy Is the Lord," "Jesus Messiah."

I can't help but think that Jesus was praying for nine-year-old Chris Tomlin.

The devil's best attempts to discourage us fall victim to God's resolve to shape us. What Satan intends for evil, Jesus will use for good. Satan's attempts to destroy us will actually develop our faith. Jesus says, "In this world you will have trouble. But take heart! I have overcome the world" (John 16:33).

Can you imagine the assurance this intercession brings? Tyler Sullivan can. When he was an eleven-year-old elementary school student, he skipped a day of class. He played hooky, not in order to hang out with friends or watch television; he missed school so he could meet the president of the United States.

Barack Obama was visiting Tyler's hometown of Golden Valley, Minnesota. His father had introduced the president at an event. After the speech when Tyler met the president, Obama realized that Tyler was missing school. He asked an aide to fetch him a card with presidential letterhead. He asked for the name of Tyler's teacher. He then wrote a note: "Please excuse Tyler. He was with me. Barack Obama, the president."[3]

I'm thinking the teacher read the note and granted the request. It's not every day the president speaks up on behalf of a kid.

But every day Jesus speaks up for you. "He always lives to intercede for [us]" (Heb. 7:25). For People of the Promise, Jesus is praying. In the midst of your storm, he is praying for you.

And through the mist of your storm, he is coming. "Shortly before dawn Jesus went out to them, walking on the lake. When the disciples saw him walking on the lake, they were terrified. 'It's a ghost,' they said, and cried out in fear" (Matt. 14:25–26).

Jesus became the answer to his own prayer.

He turned the water into a walkway. He who made the Red Sea become two walls for Moses and made the iron ax-head swim for Elisha transformed the water of Galilee into a level path and came walking to the apostles in the storm.

The followers panicked. They never expected to see Jesus in the squall.

Neither did Nika Maples. She thought she was all alone. Lupus had ravaged her body, slurred her speech, and blurred her sight. She could not walk, sit up, or move. She could eat only the smallest of bites. She breathed in gasps and spurts. Sleep came stubbornly if at all. The doctors were bewildered, and Nika's family was terrified. She was only twenty years old, and her body was shutting down.

By the time she was admitted into the ICU of a hospital in Fort Worth, Texas, doctors were beginning to fear for her survival. On one particularly difficult night, she couldn't sleep at all. She knew she would rest better if someone held her hand. But since she couldn't speak, she had no way to ask for comfort. Her mother was in the room, but Nika could tell by her breathing that she had dozed off. Nika began to pray: *God, I need You. I can't go to sleep tonight . . . Will you please send someone to hold my hand? I can't tell anyone what I need, can't ask anyone. Will you please just tell Mom or a nurse or somebody to hold my hand?*

Minutes passed slowly. The rotating mattress rolled her onto her side and then returned her to her back. As it did, someone walked into the room.

"The scent of his skin was unfamiliar, but clearly there were soft masculine tones. His steps made no noise; Mother did not even stir. . . . [He] took my right hand, holding it warmly. I tried to open my eyes, but could not."

Nika drifted off to sleep. When she awoke, he was still holding her hand. Her mother slept across the room. Nika tried again to open her eyes to see her new friend. This time she succeeded. Through blurred vision she looked. No one was there. At that moment the pressure on her hand was gone.

She is convinced Christ was with her.[4]

He did for her what he did for the disciples. He came for her in the storm.

His followers called him a ghost, but Jesus still came. Peter's faith became fear, but Jesus still walked on the water. The winds howled and raged, but Jesus was not distracted from his mission. He stayed on course until his point was made: he is sovereign over all storms. The disciples, for the first time in Scripture, worshipped him.

"Truly you are the Son of God" (Matt. 14:33).

With a stilled boat as their altar and beating hearts as their liturgy, they worshipped Jesus.

May you and I do the same.

CHAPTER 9

No Condemnation

GOD'S PROMISE

There is now no condemnation for
those who are in Christ Jesus.

—Romans 8:1

N ew York City.
　　If you want a view of the skyline, visit the Brooklyn Bridge. For entertainment go to Broadway.

Looking for inspiration? Tour the Statue of Liberty.

Like to shop? The stores on Fifth Avenue await your credit card.

But if you want to be depressed, utterly overwhelmed, and absolutely distraught, take a cab to the corner of Avenue of the Americas and West Forty-Fourth Street and spend a few moments in the presence of the US National Debt Clock. The sign is twenty-five feet wide, weighs fifteen hundred pounds, and uses 306 bulbs to constantly, mercilessly, endlessly declare the US debt and each family's share. The original clock wasn't built to run backward, but that feature has seldom been needed. Plans to install an updated model that can display some quadrillion dollars have been discussed.[1] If debt is a tidal wave, according to this sign the undertow is going to suck us out to sea.

I'm not an economist; I'm a preacher. But my monetary experience has taught me this: when people owe more than they own, expect trouble.

Again, I'm not an economist. I'm a preacher, which may explain the odd question that occurred to me as I pondered the debt clock. What if heaven had one of these? A marquee that measured, not our fiscal debt, but our spiritual one? Scripture often refers to sin in financial terminology. Jesus taught us to pray, "Forgive us our debts" (Matt. 6:12). If sin is a debt, do you and I have a dot matrix trespass counter in heaven? Does it click at each infraction?

We lie. *Click.*

———

We gossip. *Click.*

We demand our way. *Click.*

We doze off while reading a Lucado book. *Click, click, click.*

Talk about depressing. A financial liability is one matter, but a spiritual one? The debt of sin has a serious consequence. It separates us from God.

> Your iniquities have separated
> > you from your God;
> your sins have hidden his face from you,
> > so that he will not hear. (Isa. 59:2)

The algebra of heaven reads something like this: heaven is a perfect place for perfect people, which leaves us in a perfect mess. According to heaven's debt clock we owe more than we could ever repay. Every day brings more sin, more debt, and more questions like this one: "Who will deliver me?" (Rom. 7:24 NKJV).

The realization of our moral debt sends some people into a frenzy of good works. Life becomes an unending quest to do enough, be better, accomplish more. A pursuit of piety. We attend church, tend to the sick, go on pilgrimages, and go on fasts. Yet deep within is the gnawing fear, *What if, having done all that, I've not done enough?*

Other people respond to the list, not with activity, but unbelief. They throw up their hands and walk away exasperated. No God would demand so much. He can't be pleased. He can't be satisfied. He must not exist. If he does exist, he is not worth knowing.

Two extremes. The legalist and the atheist. The worker desperate to impress God. The unbeliever convinced there is no God. Can you relate to either of the two? Do you know the weariness that comes from legalism? Do you know the loneliness that comes from atheism?

What do we do? Are despair and disbelief the only options?

No one loved to answer that question more than the apostle Paul, who said, "There is now no condemnation for those who are in Christ Jesus" (Rom. 8:1).

How could he say this? Had he not seen the debt we owe? He'd certainly seen his own. Paul entered the pages of Scripture as Saul, the self-professed Pharisee of all Pharisees and the most religious man in town. But all his scruples and law keeping hadn't made him a better person. He was bloodthirsty and angry, determined to extinguish anything and everyone Christian.

His attitude began to change on the road to Damascus. That's when Jesus appeared to him in the desert, knocked him off his high horse, and left him sightless for three days. Paul could see only one direction: inward. And what he saw he did not like. He saw a narrow-minded tyrant. During the time of blindness, God gave him a vision that a man named Ananias would restore his sight. So when Ananias did, Paul "got up and was baptized" (Acts 9:18).

Within a few days he was preaching about Christ. Within a few years he was off on his first missionary journey. Within a couple of decades he was writing the letters we still read today, each one of which makes the case for Christ and the cross.

We aren't told when Paul realized the meaning of grace. Was it immediately on the Damascus road? Or gradually during the three-day darkness? Or after Ananias restored his sight? We aren't told. But we know that Paul got grace. Or grace got Paul. Either way, he embraced the improbable offer that God would make us right with him through Jesus Christ. Paul's logic followed a simple outline:

Our debt is enough to sink us.

God loves us too much to leave us.

So God has found a way to save us.

Paul began his case for Christ by describing our problem: "For all have sinned and fall short of the glory of God" (Rom. 3:23). We haven't met the standard God set. We were intended to bear the nature of God. To speak, act, and behave the way he speaks, acts, and behaves. To love as he loves. To value what he values. To honor those he honors. This is the glorious standard God has set. We have failed to meet it. Jesus, on the other hand, succeeded. "Christ never sinned" (2 Cor. 5:21 NLV).

What a remarkable statement! Not once did Jesus turn right when he was supposed to turn left. He never stayed silent when he was supposed to speak, or spoke when he was supposed to stay silent. He was "tempted in every way, just as we are—yet he did not sin" (Heb. 4:15). He was the image of God twenty-four hours a day, seven days a week.

When it comes to the standard, he is the standard. To be sinless is to be like Jesus.

But who can?

We may have occasional moments of goodness, deeds of kindness, but who among us reflects the image of God all day every day? Paul couldn't find anyone. "As it is written: 'There is no one righteous, not even one; there is no one who understands; there is no one who seeks God'" (Rom. 3:10–11).

People often bristle at the message of this verse. They take offense at its allegation. No one is righteous? No one seeks God? And then they produce their résumés of righteousness. They pay taxes. They love their families. They avoid addiction. They give to the poor. They seek justice for the oppressed. Compared to the rest of the world, they are good people.

Ah, but herein lies the problem. Our standard is not the rest of the world. Our standard is Christ. Compared to Christ, we, well . . . Can you hear the debt clock?

Sometime ago I took up swimming for exercise. I didn't buy a Speedo, but I did buy some goggles, went to a pool, and gave it a go. Over the weeks I gradually progressed from a tadpole to a small frog.

I'm not much to look at, but I can get up and down the lane. In fact, I was beginning to feel pretty good about my progress.

So good, in fact, that when Josh Davis invited me to swim with him, I accepted. You remember Josh Davis, three-time gold medalist in the Atlanta Olympics. His waist size is my thigh size. Half of his warm-up is my entire workout. He is as comfortable in a swimming lane as most of us are in a cafeteria line.

So when he offered to give me some pointers, I jumped in the pool. (A pool, incidentally, that bears the name Josh Davis Natatorium.) After all, I had two months of swimming experience under my belt . . . Senior Olympics? Who knows? So with Josh in his lane and me next to him in mine, he suggested, "Let's swim two laps and see how fast you go." Off I went. I gave it all I had. I was surprised at the finish to see that he had touched the wall only seconds before me. I felt pretty good about myself. I half expected to see photographers and endorsers gathered on the edge of the pool.

"Have you been here long?" I panted.

"Just a few seconds."

"You mean I finished only a few seconds behind you?"

"That's right."

Whoa . . . Forget Senior Olympics. I'm thinking world-record holder. But then Josh added, "There was one difference. While you swam two laps, I swam six."

Josh raised the bar. He displayed swimming at the highest level.

On a minute scale he did in the pool what Jesus did for humanity. Jesus demonstrated what a godly life looks like.

So what are we to do? He is holy; we are not. He is perfect; we are not. His character is flawless; ours is flawed. A yawning canyon separates us from God. Might we hope that God will overlook it? He would, except for one essential detail. He is a God of justice. If he does not punish sin, he is not just. If he is not just, then what hope do we have of a just heaven? The next life will be occupied by sinners who found a loophole, who skirted the system. Yet if God punishes us for our sin, then we are lost. So what is the solution? Again we turn to Paul for the explanation:

> What does Scripture say? "Abraham believed God, and it was credited to him as righteousness."
>
> Now to the one who works, wages are not credited as a gift but as an obligation. However, to the one who does not work but trusts God who justifies the ungodly, their faith is credited as righteousness. (Rom. 4:3–5)

To credit something is to make payment for it. I have a credit card. If I were to write a check to pay the balance on the card, the debt on the card would be removed, and I would be credited a zero balance. I would have no debt. No outstanding payment. No obligation. None whatsoever.

According to Paul, God has done the same with our spiritual debt. He presents Abraham as an example of a grace recipient. Yes, Abraham from 2000 BC! Abraham had, not a credit-card debt, but a spiritual debt. He had sinned. He was a good man, I am certain, but not good enough to live debt-free. His debt clock had abundant clicks.

Every time he cursed his camel. *Click.*
Every time he flirted with a handmaiden. *Click.*
Every time he wondered where in the world God was leading him
 and if God knew where in the world he was headed. *Click. Click.*
 Click.

But for all the bad things Abraham did, there was one good thing he chose to do. He believed. He put his faith in God. And because he believed, a wonderful, unspeakably great thing happened to his debt clock.

It was returned to zero!

"Abraham believed God, and it was credited to him as righteousness." God's promise to Abraham was salvation by faith. God's promise to you and me is salvation by faith. Just faith.

> God sacrificed Jesus on the altar of the world to clear that world of sin. Having faith in him sets us in the clear. God decided on this course of action in full view of the public—to set the world in the clear with himself through the sacrifice of Jesus, finally taking care of the sins he had so patiently endured. This is not only clear, but it's *now*—this is current history! God sets things right. He also makes it possible for us to live in his rightness. (Rom. 3:25–26 THE MESSAGE)

God never compromised his standard. He satisfied every demand of justice. Yet he also gratified the longing of love. Too just to overlook our sin, too loving to dismiss us, he placed our sin on his Son and punished it there. "God put the wrong on him who never did anything wrong, so we could be put right with God" (2 Cor. 5:21 THE MESSAGE).

Now we understand the cry of Christ from the cross: "My God, my God, why have you forsaken me?" (Matt. 27:46).

Jesus felt the wrath of a just and holy God.

Wave after wave. Load after load. Hour after hour. He cried out the words of the psalm he would have known since his youth: "Why have you forsaken me?" He felt the separation between his Father and him.

And then when he could scarcely take any more, he cried, "It is finished!" (John 19:30 NASB). His mission was complete.

At the moment of Jesus' death, an unbelievable miracle occurred. "Jesus cried out with a loud voice, and breathed His last. Then the veil of the temple was torn in two from top to bottom" (Mark 15:37–38 NKJV). According to Henry and Richard Blackaby, "The veil separated the people from the temple's Most Holy Place, and it had done so for centuries. According to tradition, the veil—a handbreadth in thickness—was woven of seventy-two twisted plaits, each plait consisting of twenty-four threads. The veil was apparently sixty feet long and thirty feet wide."[2]

We aren't talking about small, delicate drapes. This curtain was a wall made of fabric. The fact that it was torn from top to bottom reveals that the hands behind the deed were divine. God himself grasped the curtain and ripped it in two.

No more!

No more division. No more separation. No more sacrifices. "No condemnation for those who are in Christ Jesus" (Rom. 8:1).

> [Jesus] personally carried our sins
>> in his body on the cross
> so that we can be dead to sin
>> and live for what is right.
> By his wounds
>> you are healed. (1 Peter 2:24 NLT)

Heaven's work of redemption was finished. Christ's death brought new life. Whatever barrier that had separated—or might ever separate—us from God was gone.

Gone is the fear of falling short! Gone is the anxious quest for right behavior. Gone are the nagging questions: Have I done enough? Am I good enough? Will I achieve enough? The legalist finds rest. The atheist finds hope. The God of Abraham is not a God of burdens but a God of rest. He knows we are made of flesh. He knows we cannot achieve perfection. The God of the Bible is the One who says:

———

Come to me, all you who are weary and burdened, and I will give you rest. Take my yoke upon you and learn from me, for I am gentle and humble in heart, and you will find rest for your souls. For my yoke is easy and my burden is light. (Matt. 11:28–30)

When you lose your temper with your child, Christ intervenes. "I paid for that." When you tell a lie and all of heaven groans, your Savior speaks up: "My death covered that sin." As you lust over someone's centerfold, gloat over someone's pain, covet someone's success, or cuss someone's mistake, Jesus stands before the tribunal of heaven and points to the blood-streaked cross. "I've already made provision. I've paid that debt. I've taken away the sins of the world."

Karl Barth described grace in this manner:

On the one side there is God in His glory as Creator and Lord. . . . And on the other side there is man, not merely the creature, but the sinner, the one who exists in the flesh and who in the flesh is in opposition to Him. It is not merely a frontier, but a yawning abyss. Yet this abyss is crossed, not by man, not by both God and man, but only by God. . . . This man does not even know how it comes about or happens to him.[3]

Salvation, from beginning to end, is a work of our Father. God does not stand on a mountain and tell us to climb it and find him. He comes down into our dark valley and finds us. He does not offer to pay all the debt minus a dollar if we'll pay the dollar. He pays every penny. He doesn't offer to complete the work if we will start it. He does all the work, from beginning to end. He does not bargain with us, telling us to clean up our lives so he can help. He washes our sins without our help.

An elderly woman was once asked about the security of her salvation. Though she'd dedicated her life to the Lord, a cynic asked, "How can you be sure? How can you know that after all these years God won't let you sink into hell?"

"He would lose more than I would," she replied. "All I would lose would be my own soul. He would lose his good name."

What a gift God has given you. You've won the greatest lottery in the history of humanity, and you didn't even pay for the ticket! Your soul is secure, your salvation guaranteed. Your name is written in the only book that matters. You're only a few sand grains in the hourglass from a tearless, graveless, painless existence.

This is the message of God, the promise of grace. The declaration Paul preached with unwearied enthusiasm: "What we cannot do, God has done. He justifies us by his grace." Grace is entirely God's. God loving. God stooping. God offering. God caring and God carrying.

This is God's version of grace. Is it yours? Don't hurry too quickly past that question. Guilt simmers like a toxin in far too many souls. Do not let it have a place in yours. Before you turn the page, internalize this promise that is written with the crimson blood of Christ: "There is now no condemnation for those who are in Christ Jesus" (Rom. 8:1).

No condemnation. Not "limited condemnation," "appropriate condemnation," or "calculated condemnation." That is what people give people. What does God give his children? "No condemnation."

Stand on this promise. Or, better said, take this promise to the clock, your personal debt clock. As you look up at the insurmountable debt you owe, the debt you can never pay, let this promise be declared: "There is now no condemnation for those who are in Christ Jesus."

CHAPTER 10

This Temporary Tomb

GOD'S PROMISE

Death has been swallowed up in victory.

—1 Corinthians 15:54

Several years ago I received an urgent call to visit a dying man in the hospital. I didn't know Peter well, but I knew that he was paying a high price for his hard living. Years of drugs and alcohol abuse had perforated his system. Though he'd made peace with God through Christ, his liver was in conflict with his body.

When his ex-wife phoned me, she was standing at his bedside. Peter, she explained, was knocking at death's door. Though I hurried, he entered it minutes before I arrived. The hospital-room atmosphere had a "just happened" feel to it. She was still standing by the bed. His hair was stroked back from her touch. The lipstick imprint of a kiss was just below the dorsal knuckles on his left hand. Perspiration beads sparkled on his forehead.

She saw me enter and looked up. With eyes and words she explained, "He just left."

Peter silently slipped out. Exited. Departed. One moment here. The next moment . . . where? He passed, not away, but on. Yet on to where? And in what form? To what place? In what manner? And, once there, what did he see? What did he know or do? We so desire to understand.

Who in your life "just left"? When the breathing of your spouse ceased, the beating heart in your womb stopped, the beep of your grandmother's monitor became a flat-lined tone, what happened in that moment?

And what will happen to you in yours? Barring the return of Christ, you will have one . . . a last gasp, a final pulse. Your lungs will empty and blood will still. What will we be after we die? Answers vary.

- Nothing, some people say. We will decay and disintegrate. Death is a dead end. Our works and reputation might survive but not us.
- Ghosts perhaps? Phantoms of what we once were. Pale as a snow-drift. As structured as a morning mist. What will we be after we die? Specters.
- Or hawks. Or cows. Or a car mechanic in Kokomo. Reincarnation rewards or punishes us according to our behavior. We come back to earth in another mortal body.
- Or a part of the universe. Eternity absorbs us like a lake absorbs a raindrop. We return to what we were before we were what we are . . . We return to the cosmic consciousness of the universe.

Christianity, on the other hand, posits a new, startling idea. "Death has been swallowed up in victory" (1 Cor. 15:54). The cemetery is less a place of loss and more a place of gain. The dead in Christ are to be mourned, for sure. But they are also to be envied. Funeral dirges are understandable, but a trumpet blast would be equally appropriate.

According to the promise of the empty tomb, my friend Peter awoke in a world so wondrously better than this one that it would take God himself to convince him to return to earth. We know this because Jesus' miracles included only three resurrections. I'm thinking he had a hard time getting return guests.

People of the Promise hold on to the unshakable hope that hinges on the resurrection of Christ. The Christian hope depends entirely upon the assumption that Jesus Christ died a physical death, vacated an actual grave, and ascended into heaven where he, at this moment, reigns as head of the church.

The resurrection changed everything.

It was Sunday morning after the Friday execution. The sky was dark. The disciples had scattered. And the Roman executioner was wondering about breakfast or work or his next day off. But he was not wondering about the fellow he had nailed to a cross and pierced with a spear. Jesus was dead and buried. Yesterday's news, right?

Wrong.

There was a violent earthquake, for an angel of the Lord came down from heaven and, going to the tomb, rolled back the stone and sat on it. His appearance was like lightning, and his clothes were white as snow. The guards were so afraid of him that they shook and became like dead men.

The angel said to the women, "Do not be afraid, for I know that you are looking for Jesus, who was crucified. He is not here; he has risen, just as he said. Come and see the place where he lay." (Matt. 28:2–6)

Had such words never been spoken, had the body of Jesus decayed into dust in the borrowed tomb, you would not be reading these pages, and we would not be discussing this promise. But the words were spoken, and the promise was made.

Jesus went on a resurrection tour. He appeared to the women near the tomb. He appeared to the followers in the Upper Room. He appeared to the disciples on the road to Emmaus. He appeared to his friends on the shore of Galilee. He spoke with them. He ate with them. They touched his body; they heard his words. They were convinced this Jesus was raised from the dead.

They also believed his resurrection is the preview and promise of ours. What God did for him, he will do for us. When Jesus rose from the dead, he was the "firstfruits" (1 Cor. 15:20, 23). "Firstfruits" is the first taste of the harvest. The farmer can anticipate the nature of the crop by sampling the first batch. We can anticipate our own resurrection by viewing the resurrection of Christ. What will happen when you die? Scripture reveals some intriguing assurances.

Your spirit will immediately enter into the presence of God. You will enjoy conscious fellowship with the Father and with those who have gone before. Your body will join you later. We believe this to be true because of verses like this one: "We are confident, I say, and would prefer to be away from the body and at home with the Lord" (2 Cor. 5:8).

When Peter's ex-wife asked me what happened to her husband, I could rightly say, "He is away from his body and at home with the Lord."

Isn't this the promise Jesus gave the thief on the cross? "Today you will be with me in paradise" (Luke 23:43). "Today," Christ promised. No delay. No pause. No purgatory cleansing or soul sleeping. The thief closed his eyes on earth and awoke in paradise. The soul of the believer journeys home, while the body of the believer awaits the resurrection.

My friend Luis took this journey. For the last couple of years, he greeted me at the convenience store where he worked and I bought morning coffee. He was such a kind, gentle soul. Even when his heart deteriorated, his hope never did. Last week his heart gave out. He coded three times. The medical team was able to revive him twice. After the first event, his wife was ushered into the room. Whatever Luis had seen caused him to whisper to her: *"Ven conmigo, está muy bonito."* (Come with me, it's very beautiful.)

Paradise is the first stage of heaven.

But paradise is not the final version of heaven or the ultimate expression of home.

The final age will begin when Christ returns on the final day. "For the Lord Himself will descend from heaven with a shout" (1 Thess. 4:16 NKJV). Before you see angels, hear trumpets, or embrace your grandparents, you will be engulfed by Jesus' voice. "The LORD will roar from on high" (Jer. 25:30).

He will awaken the body and summon the soul of the dead man. "The dead will hear the voice of the Son of God. . . . [A]ll who are . . .

in their graves will hear his voice. Then they will come out" (John 5:25, 28–29 NCV). He who created us will collect us. "The LORD, who scattered his people, will gather them" (Jer. 31:10 NLT).

I've stood in cemeteries and attempted to imagine this moment. The road on which Denalyn and I take our walks is marked by a small country graveyard. The headstones are faded beyond recognition. No dirt has been turned for a century. The few discernible names share a last name. I assume a family is buried there. It is just one of the millions of burial spots around the planet. Yet if these words from Jeremiah are true, it will someday witness a miracle beyond words. The same God who shook the tomb of Joseph of Arimathea will shake the soil of this simple cemetery. The grass will be pushed back from within. The caskets will open, and the bodies of these forgotten farmers will be called into the sky.

But in what form? How will the bodies look? In what shape will they appear? They are decayed, some to dust. They were wracked by disease and deformity. Some were riddled with bullets or destroyed by fire. How will these bodies be worthy of heaven?

Here is Paul's answer.

The body that is sown is perishable, it is raised imperishable; it is sown in dishonor, it is raised in glory; it is sown in weakness, it is raised in power; it is sown a natural body, it is raised a spiritual body.

If there is a natural body, there is also a spiritual body. (1 Cor. 15:42–44)

Spirits will be reunited with bodies, resulting in a spiritual body. Just as a seed becomes a plant, this fleshly body will become a spiritual body. You are going to love yours.

You've never seen yourself at your best. Even on your good days, you've been subject to bacteria, weariness, and wounds. You've never known yourself as God intended. But you will! Try to imagine a body with no pain, a mind with no wandering thoughts. Envision yourself as you were meant to be: completely whole.

And while your imagination is warmed up, envision this earth as it was intended to be: completely calm. "The wolf will live with the lamb, the leopard will lie down with the goat, the calf and the lion and the yearling together; and a little child will lead them" (Isa. 11:6). Lions won't snarl. Bears won't maim. No one, no thing, will rebel. The next age will be calm because it gladly defers to God.

"No longer will there be any curse" (Rev. 22:3). No more struggle with the earth. No more shame before God. No more tension between people. No more death. No more curse. The removal of the curse will return God's people and the universe to their intended states. Satan, the tempter, will be thrown "into the eternal fire prepared for the devil and his angels" (Matt. 25:41 ESV).

In that moment "Death is swallowed up in victory" (1 Cor. 15:54 NKJV).

Make this promise one of the blocks in your foundation. View death through the lens of Christ's resurrection. The grave brings sorrow, for sure. But it need not bring despair. The tomb could not hold Christ, and since Christ is in you, you will not long be in your tomb. "In keeping with his promise we are looking forward to a new heaven and a new earth, where righteousness dwells" (2 Peter 3:13).

This is God's promise. He will reclaim his creation. He is a God of restoration, not destruction. He is a God of *re*newal, *re*demption, *re*generation, *re*surrection. God loves to *re*do and *re*store.

"I am making everything new!" he announced (Rev. 21:5). Everything new. The old will be gone. Gone with hospital waiting rooms. Gone with tear-stained divorce papers. Gone with motionless ultrasounds. Gone with loneliness, foreclosure notices, and abuse. Gone with cancer. God will lay hold of every atom, emotion, insect, animal, and galaxy. He will reclaim every diseased body and afflicted mind. *I am making all things new.*

In the movie *As Good As It Gets*, Jack Nicholson portrays a curmudgeonly New York City author who snaps at anything that moves. He is rich, lonely, bitter, and afraid. He has phobias like the Amazon has piranhas, and they gnaw on him. He fears stepping on sidewalk cracks, using a bar of soap twice, and shaking hands with anyone. He always eats in the same restaurant at the same table and orders the same meal from the same server.

At one point his neurosis reaches a breaking point, and he goes to see his psychoanalyst. He sees the waiting room of patients and sighs. He avoids physical contact but can't avoid the impact of the sad collection of misery. "Is this as good as it gets?" he asks.

Many people assume that it is. They mistakenly think that their fondest moment, deepest joy, and most profound experience happen sometime between the delivery room and the funeral home. Someone needs to tell them this is just the beginning. As good as it gets? For the Christian this world is as bad as it gets.

Can I urge, beg, and implore you to set your heart on this hope? "Since we are receiving a kingdom that cannot be shaken" (Heb. 12:28), we can have a hope that won't be shaken. Set your heart and eyes on it.

> So we do not give up. Our physical body is becoming older and weaker, but our spirit inside us is made new every day. We have small troubles for a while now, but they are helping us gain an eternal glory that is much greater than the troubles. We set our eyes not on what we see but on what we cannot see. What we see will last only a short time, but what we cannot see will last forever. (2 Cor. 4:16–18 NCV)

The verb used in the phrase "set our eyes" is *skopeó*, the great-grandfather of the English word *scope*. When you press your eye against the scope of a rifle, what happens? All your gaze is focused on one item. Lift up your eyes and look, long and hard, at the promised heaven.

Let this hope for tomorrow bring strength to today. Your finest moment will be your final moment! I know, most people say otherwise. Death is to be avoided, postponed, and ignored. But they do not have what you have. You have a promise from the living God. Your death will be swallowed up in victory! Jesus Christ rose from the dead, not just to show you his power, but also to reveal your path. He will lead you through the valley of death.

Several weeks ago I spent an hour in the office of a cemetery director. Yet another birthday had reminded me that the day of my departure is increasingly near. It seemed right to me to make burial preparations. Then again, it didn't. (Especially when I learned the cost of the plots!)

As the gentleman was showing me the cemetary map and the available sections, I had an idea. "You'll likely think I'm crazy," I told him, "but can I record a message for my tombstone? A sort of voice mail for the grave."

To his credit he didn't call me crazy and promised to check. Within a few days he gave me the good news. "Yes, it is possible. A recorded message can be encased in the grave marker. At the push of the button, a message can be played."

I thanked him and got to work. Within a few minutes I had mine written. It's not yet recorded. Perhaps I can test it with you first.

The granite stone will contain a button and an invitation: "Press for a word from Max." If you do, this is what you will hear.

Thanks for coming by. Sorry you missed me. I'm not here. I'm home. Finally home. At some point my King will call, and this grave will be shown for the temporary tomb it is. You might want to step to the side in case that happens while you are here. Again, I appreciate the visit. Hope you've made plans for your own departure. All the best, Max.

Yeah, it still needs some work. While the wording might change, the promise never will: "Death has been swallowed up in victory" (1 Cor. 15:54).

CHAPTER 11

Joy Is Soon Coming

GOD'S PROMISE

Weeping may last through the night,
but joy comes with the morning.

—Psalm 30:5 NLT

Amanda Todd was the Canadian teenager who became an unwitting spokesperson for despair at the age of fifteen after a predator had convinced her to pose topless for a photo. He later blackmailed her with threats to circulate the picture if she didn't reveal more, but he posted the photo anyway. Humiliation rained down on her like a summer squall. From the high school hallway to the Internet highway, she became the laughingstock of her circle.

Already a fragile and private person, she retreated even further. She avoided friends, stayed home. Still, she couldn't escape the texts, calls, and stares. The family changed schools, but the mockery followed. For three years she was stalked and taunted. She descended into drugs and alcohol. She cut herself. She hid in her room. She drank bleach and tried to take her life. Finally, in an act of desperation, she posted a nine-minute video on YouTube. Using flash cards set to a maudlin song, she recounted her months of horror: the shame she brought on her family, the pain she brought on herself. The video image shows only the lower half of her face and the written messages.

I have nobody.
I need someone.
My name is Amanda Todd.

A month after posting the video, she attempted suicide again. This time she succeeded.[1]

If hope were a rain cloud, Amanda Todd lived in the Sahara desert.

She searched the skies for a reason to live and found none. Does God have a promise for someone like her?

He'd better. Anyone can give pep talks, but if God is who he claims to be, he sure as shootin' better have a word for the despondent. Self-help manuals might get you through a bad mood or a tough patch. But what about an abusive childhood or a debilitating accident or years of chronic pain or public ridicule? Does God have a word for the dark nights of the soul?

He does. The promise begins with this phrase: "Weeping may last through the night" (Ps. 30:5 NLT).

Of course, you knew that much. You didn't need to read the verse to know its truth. Weeping can last through the night. Just ask the widow in the cemetery or the mother in the emergency room. The man who lost his job can tell you. So can the teenager who lost her way. Weeping may last through the night, and the next night, and the next.

This is not new news to you.

But this may be: "Joy comes with the morning" (Ps. 30:5 NLT). Despair will not rule the day. Sorrow will not last forever. The clouds may eclipse the sun, but they cannot eliminate it. Night might delay the dawn, but it cannot defeat it. Morning comes. Not as quickly as we want. Not as dramatically as we desire. But morning comes, and with it comes joy.

Do you need this promise? Have you wept a river? Have you forsaken hope? Do you wonder if a morning will ever bring this night to an end? Mary Magdalene did.

In the forest of the New Testament, she is the weeping willow. She is the one upon whom tragedy cast its coldest winter. Before she knew Jesus, she had seven demons (Luke 8:2). She was a prisoner of seven afflictions. What might this list include? Depression? Loneliness? Shame? Fear? Perhaps she was a recluse or a prostitute. Maybe she'd been abused, abandoned. The number seven is sometimes used in the

Bible to describe completeness. It could be that Mary Magdalene was completely consumed with troubles.

But then something happened. Jesus stepped into her world. He spoke and the demons fled. For the first time in a long time, the oppressive forces were gone. Banished. Evicted. Mary Magdalene could sleep well, eat enough, and smile again. The face in the mirror wasn't anguished.

Jesus restored life to her life.

She reciprocated. She was among the female followers who "were contributing from their own resources to support Jesus and his disciples" (Luke 8:3 NLT). Wherever Jesus went, Mary Magdalene followed. She heard him teach. She saw him perform miracles. She helped pay expenses. She may have even prepared his meals. She was always near Christ.

Even at his crucifixion. She stood "near the cross" (John 19:25).

When they pounded the nails in his hands, she heard the hammer. When they pierced his side with a spear, she saw the blood. When they lowered his body from the cross, she was there to help prepare it for burial.

On Friday Mary Magdalene watched Jesus die.

On Saturday she observed a sad Sabbath.

When Sunday came, Mary Magdalene went to the tomb to finish the work she had begun on Friday. "Early on the first day of the week, Mary Magdalene went to the tomb while it was still dark" (John 20:1 NCV). She knew nothing of the empty tomb. She came with no other motive than to wash the remaining clots of blood from his beard and say goodbye.

It was a dark morning.

When she arrived at the tomb, the bad news became worse. Mary Magdalene "saw that the stone had been taken away" (v. 1 NKJV). Assuming that grave robbers had taken the body, she hurried back down the trail until she found Peter and John. "They have taken away the Lord out of the tomb" (v. 2 NASB), she told them.

Peter and John ran to the grave site. John was faster, but Peter was bolder. He stepped inside. John followed him. Peter saw the empty slab and stared. But John saw the empty slab and believed. The evidence all came together for him: the resurrection prophecies, the removed stone, the linen wrappings, the head cloth folded and placed. John did the math. No one took Jesus' body. No one robbed the grave. Jesus rose from the dead. John looked and believed. Easter had its first celebrant.

Peter and John hurried to tell the others. We expect the camera lens of the gospel to follow them. After all, they were apostles, future authors of epistles. They compose two-thirds of the inner circle. We expect John to describe what the apostles did next. He doesn't. He tells the story of the one who remained behind.

"But Mary stood outside by the tomb weeping" (v. 11 NKJV).

Her face was awash with tears. Her shoulders heaved with sobs. She felt all alone. It was just Mary Magdalene, her despair, and a vacant tomb. "As she wept she stooped down and looked into the tomb. And she saw two angels in white sitting, one at the head and the other at the feet, where the body of Jesus had lain. Then they said to her, 'Woman, why are you weeping?'" (vv. 11–13 NKJV).

Mary Magdalene mistook the angels for men. It's easy to imagine why. It was still dark outside, even darker in the tomb. Her eyes were tear filled. She had no reason to think angels would be in the tomb. Bone diggers? Maybe. Caretakers? Possibly. But her Sunday was too dark to expect the presence of angels. "They have taken away my Lord, and I do not know where they have laid Him" (v. 13 NKJV).

Mary's world had officially hit rock bottom. Her master murdered. His body buried in a borrowed grave. His tomb robbed. His body stolen. Now two strangers were sitting on the slab where his body had been laid. Sorrow intermingled with anger.

Have you ever had a moment like this? A moment in which bad news became worse? In which sadness wrapped around you like a fog? In which you came looking for God yet couldn't find him?

Maybe Mary Magdalene's story is your story. If so, you're going to love what happened next. In the midst of Mary's darkest moment, the Son came out.

> Now when she had said this, she turned around and saw Jesus standing there, and did not know that it was Jesus. Jesus said to her, "Woman, why are you weeping? Whom are you seeking?"
>
> She, supposing Him to be the gardener, said to Him, "Sir, if You have carried Him away, tell me where You have laid Him, and I will take Him away." (vv. 14–15 NKJV)

She didn't recognize her Lord. So Jesus did something about it. He called her by name. "Jesus said to her, 'Mary!'" (v. 16 NKJV).

Maybe it was the way he said it. The inflection. The tone. The Galilean accent. Maybe it was the memory associated with it, the moment she first heard someone say her name unladen with perversion or an agenda.

"Mary."

When she heard him call her by name, she knew the source. "She turned and said to Him, 'Rabboni!' (which is to say, Teacher)" (v. 16 NKJV). In a second. In a pivot of the neck. In the amount of time it took her to rotate her head from this way to that, her world went from a dead Jesus to a living one. Weeping may last through the night, but joy . . .

She took hold of him. We know this to be true because of the next words Jesus said: "Don't hold on to me, because I have not yet gone up to the Father" (v. 17 NCV).

Maybe she fell at his feet and held his ankles.

———

Maybe she threw her arms around his shoulders and held him close.

We don't know how she held him. We just know she did.

And Jesus let her do so. Even if the gesture lasted for only a moment, Jesus allowed it. How wonderful that the resurrected Lord was not too holy, too otherly, too divine, too supernatural to be touched.

This moment serves a sacred role in the Easter story. It, at once, reminds us that Jesus is the conquering King and the Good Shepherd. He has power over death. But he also has a soft spot for the Mary Magdalenes of the world. The regal hero is relentlessly tender.

I wish I could paint this scene. Capture it in oil on canvas and frame it. The brilliant golden sunrise. The open tomb. Angels watching from a distance. The white-robed Messiah. The joy-filled Mary. Her hands extended to him. His eyes upon her. If you are an artist and paint it, please include the reflection of the sunrise in the tears of Mary. And, by all means, paint a broad smile on the face of Jesus.

Then "Mary Magdalene came and told the disciples that she had seen the Lord, and that He had spoken these things to her" (v. 18 NKJV). To her! Of all the people to whom he could have spoken, Jesus went first to her. He'd just ripped the gates of hell off their hinges. He'd just yanked the fangs out of Satan's mouth. He'd just turned BC into AD, for heaven's sake! Jesus was the undisputed King of the universe. Ten thousand angels stood in rapt attention ready to serve. And what was his first act? To whom did he go? To Mary, the weeping, heartbroken woman who once had seven demons.

Why? Why her? As far as we know, she didn't become a missionary. No epistle bears her name. No New Testament story describes her work. Why did Jesus create this moment for Mary Magdalene? Perhaps to send this message to all the heavyhearted people: "Weeping may last through the night, but joy comes with the morning" (Ps. 30:5 NLT).

Joy comes.

Joy comes because Jesus comes. And if we don't recognize his face, he will call our names. "See, I have engraved you on the palms of my hands" (Isa. 49:16).

Your name is not buried in some heavenly file. God needs no name tag to jog his memory about you. Your name is tattooed, engraved, on his hand. He has more thoughts about you than the Pacific coast has grains of sand.

You are everything to God.

I read a story about a priest from Detroit who traveled to Ireland to visit relatives. One day he was walking the shores of Lake Killarney with his uncle. They watched the sun rise, and for a full twenty minutes the two men scarcely spoke. As they resumed their walk, the priest noticed his uncle was smiling.

"Uncle Seamus," he said, "you look very happy."

"I am."

"How come?"

"The Father of Jesus is very fond of me."[2]

He's fond of you, too, dear friend.

Do you find this hard to believe? You think I'm talking to someone else? Someone who is holier, better, nicer? Someone who didn't screw up his marriage or mess up her career? Someone who didn't get hooked on pills or porn or popularity?

I'm not. I'm talking directly to you.

I'm saying the greatest news in the world is not that God made the world but that God loves the world. He loves you. You did not earn this love. His love for you will not end if you lose your temper. His love for you will not fade if you lose your way. His love for you will not diminish if your discipline does.

You have never lived one unloved day.

Someone told you that God loves good people. Wrong. There are no good people.

———

Someone told you that God loves you if you love him first. Wrong. He loves people who have never thought of him.

Someone told you that God is ticked off, cranky, and vindictive. Wrong. We tend to be ticked off, cranky, and vindictive. But God?

> GOD is sheer mercy and grace;
>> not easily angered, he's rich in love.
> He doesn't endlessly nag and scold,
>> nor hold grudges forever.
> He doesn't treat us as our sins deserve,
>> nor pay us back in full for our wrongs.
> As high as heaven is over the earth,
>> so strong is his love to those who fear him.
> And as far as sunrise is from sunset,
>> he has separated us from our sins.
> As parents feel for their children,
>> GOD feels for those who fear him. (Ps. 103:8–13 THE MESSAGE)

God loves you, and because he does, you can be assured joy will come.

Mary Cushman learned this truth.[3] The Depression of the 1930s all but devastated her family. Her husband's average paycheck shrank to eighteen dollars a week. Since he was given to illness, there were many weeks he didn't earn even that much.

She began to take in laundry and ironing. She dressed her five kids with Salvation Army clothing. At one point the local grocer, to whom they owed fifty dollars, accused her eleven-year-old son of stealing.

That was all she could take. She said:

I couldn't see any hope. . . . I shut off my washing machine, took my little five-year-old daughter into the bedroom, and plugged up the windows and cracks with paper and rags.... I turned on the gas heater we had in the bedroom—and didn't light it. As I lay down on the bed with my daughter beside me, she said, "Mommy, this is funny—we just got up a little while ago!" But I said, "Never mind, we'll take a little nap." Then I closed my eyes, listening to the gas escape from the heater. I shall never forget the smell of that gas....

Suddenly I thought I heard music. I listened. I had forgotten to turn the radio off in the kitchen. It didn't matter now. But the music kept on, and presently I heard someone singing an old hymn:

What a Friend we have in Jesus,
All our sins and griefs to bear!
What a privilege to carry
Everything to God in prayer.
Oh, what peace we often forfeit,
Oh, what needless pains we bear,
All because we do not carry
Everything to God in prayer!

As I listened to that hymn, I realized that I had made a tragic mistake. I had tried to fight all my terrible battles alone.... I jumped up, turned off the gas, opened the door, and raised the windows.

She went on to explain how she spent the rest of the day giving thanks to God for the blessings she had forgotten: five healthy children. She promised she would never again be ungrateful. They eventually lost their home, but she never lost her hope. They weathered the Depression. Those five children grew up, married, and had children of their own.

As I look back on that terrible day when I turned on the gas, I thank God over and over that I "woke up" in time. What joys I would have missed. . . . How many wonderful years I would have forfeited forever! Whenever I hear now of someone who wants to end his life, I feel like crying out, "Don't do it! Don't!" The blackest moments we live through can only last a little time—and then comes the future.[4]

Joy comes. Watch for it. Expect it as you would the morning sunrise or the evening twilight. It came to Mary Magdalene. It came to Mary Cushman. And it will come to you, my friend.

Do what People of the Promise do. Keep coming to Jesus. Even though the trail is dark. Even though the sun seems to sleep. Even though everyone else is silent, walk to Jesus. Mary Magdalene did this. No, she didn't comprehend the promise of Jesus. She came looking for a dead Jesus, not a living one. But at least she came. And because she came to him, he came to her.

And you? You'll be tempted to give up and walk away. But don't. Even when you don't feel like it, keep walking the trail to the empty tomb. Open your Bible. Meditate on Scripture. Sing hymns. Talk to other believers. Place yourself in a position to be found by Jesus, and listen carefully. That gardener very well might be your Redeemer.

Weeping comes. It comes to all of us. Heartaches leave us with tear-streaked faces and heavy hearts. Weeping comes. But so does joy. Darkness comes, but so does the morning. Sadness comes, but so does hope. Sorrow may have the night, but it cannot have our lives.

CHAPTER 12

You Will Have Power

GOD'S PROMISE

You will receive power when the
Holy Spirit comes on you.

—Acts 1:8

I have a bargain for you to consider, a really great deal on a new tripod. It is top of the line, weather resistant, and lightweight. It folds up to fit in a backpack. It adjusts to secure any type of camera. This tripod can be a treasure that you pass down to all future photographers in your family. Interested? I'm offering it one-third off the regular price. It's only fair that I do since this tripod is missing one-third of its legs. Yes, this is a two-legged tripod. Imagine the convenience of one fewer legs to fold up and pack. No wonder it is so lightweight. Besides, who needs all three legs?

What's that? You do? You're unconvinced of the value? You'd rather wait for a three-legged tripod?

Well, okay. Then let me move on to bargain number two, a tricycle. Just think of the joy your youngster will have riding up and down the sidewalk on this spectacular trike. Fire-engine red. Tassels that dangle from the handles. And, listen to this, a little bell that sits on the handlebar. Again, a great bargain. I'm offering it at one-third the original price. With these savings you can take the entire family out to dinner! There is, however, the small matter of one missing wheel. But the trike still has two. Little Johnny will eventually need to ride a two-wheeler anyway. Might as well start him out right. Buy him this two-wheeled trike.

You're giving me that look again. You're rolling your eyes at me the way Denalyn does. Now you are sighing. Come on, don't walk away. Okay, the two-legged tripod is no good. The two-legged tricycle falls short of your expectations. But I have one more bargain for you to consider.

Have you ever seen a prism? Nothing captures the radiance of sunlight like a triangular prism. You'll spend hours caught up in rapt fascination with the refractions of this simple tool. Entertain the kids. Impress your date. Get a good grade in science class. No home is complete without a triangular prism. This one is particularly suited for the budget-minded consumer. A slight factory defect has left one side of the triangle opaque. The other two sides work fine, mind you. But one third resists the light rather than refracts it. Granted, the flaw is a slight disadvantage, but on the other hand who else on your block owns a two-sided prism? Of course, I'll lower the price by one-third to compensate for the defect.

Don't be so quick to shake your head. Think about it. One-third off the price for a tripod that is missing a leg, a trike that is missing a wheel, or a prism that is missing a side. Do you not see the value here?

Of course you don't, and I don't blame you. Who settles for two-thirds when you can have the whole?

Many Christians do. Ask a believer to answer the question "Who is God the Father?" He has a reply. Or "Describe God the Son." She will not hesitate. But if you want to see believers hem, haw, and search for words, ask, "Who is the Holy Spirit?"

Many believers settle for a two-thirds God. They rely on the Father and the Son but overlook the Holy Spirit. You wouldn't make that mistake with a tripod, trike, or prism. You certainly don't want to make that mistake with the Trinity. Your Bible refers more than a hundred times to the Holy Spirit. Jesus says more about the Holy Spirit than he does about the church or marriage. In fact, on the eve of his death, as he prepared his followers to face the future without him, he made this great and precious promise: "You will receive power when the Holy Spirit comes on you" (Acts 1:8).

Imagine all the promises Jesus could have made to the disciples but didn't. He didn't promise immediate success. He didn't promise the absence of disease or struggles. He never guaranteed a level of income or popularity. But he did promise the perpetual, empowering presence of the Holy Spirit. The Holy Spirit is central to the life of the Christian. Everything that happens from the book of Acts to the end of the book of Revelation is a result of the work of the Holy Spirit of Christ. The Spirit came alongside the disciples, indwelled them, and gave the early church the push they needed to face the challenges ahead.

Perhaps you could use a push.

Several years ago when my legs were stronger, my belly was flatter, and my ego was bigger, I let my friend Pat convince me to enter a bike race. Not just any bike race, mind you, but a race that included a one and a half mile climb up a steep hill with a gradient of 12 percent. In other words it was a tough, climb-out-of-the-saddle, set-your-thighs-on-fire, and prepare-to-suck-air-for-ten-minutes section of the race. Appropriately called the Killer Diller, it lived up to the hype.

I knew its reputation. Still, I signed up because Pat, my riding buddy, told me I could make it. Easy for Pat to say. He is fifteen years my junior and has competed since his elementary school days. He was riding in pelotons before most of us knew what they were. When I balked at the idea of completing the race, he assured me, "Believe me, Max. You will make it."

I almost didn't.

In quick fashion the riders who belonged there left those of us who didn't far behind. We, the barrel-bellied laggards, made jokes about the upcoming ascent. But we didn't joke for long. It takes wind to talk. We soon needed all the wind we could muster to climb. I pushed and huffed and puffed, and about that point the ascent began. By the time I was halfway to the top, my thighs were on fire, and I was having less-than-pleasant thoughts about my friend Patrick.

That is when I felt the push. A hand was pressing against the small of my back. I turned and looked. It was Pat! He had already completed the race. Anticipating my utter exhaustion, he had hurried back up the hill, dismounted his bike, and scurried to give me a hand. Literally. He began pushing me up the hill! (The fact that he could keep up with me tells you how slowly I was pedaling.) "I told you that you would make it," he shouted. "I came to make sure you did."

The Holy Spirit promises to do the same. After Jesus ascended into heaven, the Holy Spirit became the primary agent of the Trinity on earth. He will complete what was begun by the Father and the Son. Though all three expressions of the Godhead are active, the Spirit is taking the lead in this, the final age. The Spirit promises to give us power, unity, supervision, and holiness: P-U-S-H. Need a push?

He promises *power* to the saint. He is the animating force behind creation.

> All creatures look to you
>> to give them their food at the proper time.
> When you give it to them,
>> they gather it up;
> when you open your hand,
>> they are satisfied with good things.
> When you hide your face,
>> they are terrified;
> when you take away their breath,
>> they die and return to the dust.
> When you send your Spirit,
>> they are created,
>> and you renew the face of the ground. (Ps. 104:27–30)

Every unfolding flower is a fingerprint of God's Spirit. "If God were to withdraw his Spirit, all life would disappear and mankind would turn again to dust" (Job 34:14–15 TLB).

The Spirit of God is a life-giving force to creation and, more significantly, a midwife of new birth for the believer. Jesus told Nicodemus:

> Very truly I tell you, no one can enter the kingdom of God unless they are born of water and the Spirit. Flesh gives birth to flesh, but the Spirit gives birth to spirit. You should not be surprised at my saying, "You must be born again." The wind blows wherever it pleases. You hear its sound, but you cannot tell where it comes from or where it is going. So it is with everyone born of the Spirit. (John 3:5–8)

The Holy Spirit enters the believer upon confession of faith (Eph. 1:13). From that point forward the Christian has access to the very power and personality of God. As the Spirit has his way in the lives of believers, a transformation occurs. They begin to think the way God thinks, love the way God loves, and see the way God sees. They minister in power and pray in power and walk in power.

This power includes the gifts of the Spirit. "But the fruit of the Spirit is love, joy, peace, forbearance, kindness, goodness, faithfulness, gentleness and self-control. Against such things there is no law" (Gal. 5:22–23).

These attributes appear in the life of the saint in the same way an apple appears on the branch of an apple tree. Fruit happens as a result of relationship. Sever the branch from the tree, and forget the fruit. Yet if the branch is secured to the trunk, nutrients flow, and fruit results.

So it is with the fruit of the Holy Spirit. As our relationship with God is secured and unmarred by rebellion, sin, or stubborn behavior, we can expect a harvest of fruit. We needn't force it. But we can expect it. It simply falls to us to stay connected.

We will also enjoy some gifts of the Spirit: wisdom, teaching, healing, prophecy, and preaching (1 Cor. 12:8–10). After listing a sampling of possible gifts, the apostle Paul clarified, "All these are the work of one and the same Spirit, and he distributes them to each one, just as he determines" (v. 11).

The Holy Spirit knows each saint and knows the needs of each church. He distributes gifts according to what the church will need in a particular region and season. When gifts are active, the church is empowered to do the work for which it was intended. For this reason we do not begrudge the talents of another believer or the accomplishments of another church. Does the saxophone player envy the tuba player? Not when each musician is playing his or her unique part and following the lead of the conductor. When church members do the same, the result is power.

And the result is *unity*.

The Holy Spirit of God is the mother hen with her extended wing, urging the church to gather in safety. "Make every effort to keep the unity of the Spirit through the bond of peace" (Eph. 4:3). Saints are never told to create unity but rather to keep the unity the Spirit provides. Harmony is always an option, because the Spirit is always present. Gone is the excuse "I just can't work alongside so-and-so." Maybe you can't, but the Spirit within you can.

Fellowship is not always easy, but unity is always possible. To say otherwise is to say that the Holy Spirit cannot do what he longs to do. Anytime a church experiences fellowship, the Spirit of God is to be praised. Anytime the church experiences conflict or disunity, the Spirit of God is to be consulted.

> Just as a body, though one, has many parts, but all its many parts form one body, so it is with Christ. For we were all baptized by one Spirit so as to form one body—whether Jews or Gentiles, slave or free—and we were all given the one Spirit to drink. Even so the body is not made up of one part but of many. (1 Cor. 12:12–14)

The Holy Spirit unifies the church.

And the Holy Spirit *supervises* the church.

I used to know a fellow who supervised an apartment complex. When I asked him to describe his job, he said, "I keep the place running." The Holy Spirit does the same and more for the church. Want to see his to-do list?

- Comfort the believers (Acts 9:31).
- Guide the believer into all truth (John 16:13).
- Reveal the things that are still to come (John 16:13).
- Offer prayers of intercession (Rom. 8:26).
- Bear witness that the saint is saved (Gal. 4:6–7; Rom. 8:16).
- Attest to the presence of God with signs and miracles (Heb. 2:4; 1 Cor. 2:4; Rom. 15:18–19).
- Create a godlike atmosphere of truth (John 14:16–17), wisdom (Deut. 34:9; Isa. 11:2), and freedom (2 Cor. 3:17).

The list of his activities is varied, wonderful, and incomplete without this word: *holy*.

The Spirit of God also makes us holy. After all, is he not the *Holy Spirit*? One of his primary activities is to cleanse us from sin and to sanctify us for holy work. Paul reminded the Corinthians: "But you were washed, you were sanctified, you were justified in the name of the Lord Jesus Christ and by the Spirit of our God" (1 Cor. 6:11).

I've seen images of women washing clothes by rubbing the garments on a washboard. Perhaps the image is a good one for the work of the Holy Spirit. He rubs us until the result is a state of spotlessness. Consequently, we can stand before the presence of God.

But when the kindness and love of God our Savior appeared, he saved us, not because of righteous things we had done, but because of his mercy. He saved us through the washing of rebirth and renewal by the Holy Spirit, whom he poured out on us generously through Jesus Christ our Savior, so that, having been justified by his grace, we might become heirs having the hope of eternal life. (Titus 3:4–7)

My bicycle story had a wonderful ending. Thanks to the push from Pat, I climbed the hill, relished in the downhill conclusion, and crossed the finish line. I finished in the back of the pack, mind you, but I finished. Suppose I had refused Pat's assistance. Suppose—perish the thought—I had resisted his help. Can you imagine the folly if I'd come to a stop, dismounted, and told him, "I can do this all by myself, thank you very much." Or imagine if I'd denied his ability to help me. "This is too great for even you, Pat. No one can climb the Killer Diller hill." Worst of all, what if I had accused him of being the enemy. "You're a fraud! Get away!"

To have reacted to Pat in such a way would have been foolish.

To react in such a way to the Spirit of God would be much more so.

Paul asked the Galatian Christians, "After starting your new lives in the Spirit, why are you now trying to become perfect by your own human effort?" (Gal. 3:3 NLT). The Christians in Ephesus relied on human strength as well. Paul assured them that they had received the Spirit. "God put his special mark of ownership on you by giving you the Holy Spirit that he had promised" (Eph. 1:13 NCV). Even so, he had to urge them to "be filled with the Spirit" (Eph. 5:18). Interesting. Can a person be saved and not full of the Holy Spirit? They were in Ephesus.

And in Jerusalem. When the apostles instructed the church to select deacons, they said, "So, brothers and sisters, choose seven of your own men who are good, full of the Spirit and full of wisdom" (Acts 6:3 NCV). The fact that men "full of the Holy Spirit" (NKJV) were to be chosen suggests that men lacking in the Spirit were present. We can have the Spirit but not let the Spirit of God have us.

A while back I purchased a new cartridge for my printer. But when I used it, no letters appeared on the page. It was half an hour before I noticed the thin strip of tape covering the outlet of the cartridge. There was plenty of ink, but until the tape was removed, no impression could be made.

Is there anything in your life that needs to be removed? Any impediment to the impression of God's Spirit? We can grieve the Spirit with our angry words and rebellion (Eph. 4:30–31; Isa. 63:10) or resist the Spirit in our disobedience (Acts 7:51). We can test or conspire against the Spirit in our plotting (Acts 5:9). We can even quench the Spirit by having no regard for God's teachings. "Never damp the fire of the Spirit, and never despise what is spoken in the name of the Lord" (1 Thess. 5:19–20 PHILLIPS).

May I ask a few blunt questions? Are you persisting in disobedience? Are you refusing to forgive someone? Are you harboring hatred? Are you persisting in an adulterous relationship? Immoral activity? A dishonest practice? Are you feeding your flesh and neglecting your faith? If the answer is yes, you are quenching the Spirit within you.

Do you want his power? Direction? Strength? Then "keep in step with the Spirit" (Gal. 5:25). He is the drum major; we are the marching band. He is the sergeant; we are the platoon. He directs and leads; we obey and follow.

Here is a cue that helps me stay in step with the Spirit. We know that the "fruit of the Spirit is love, joy, peace, patience, kindness, goodness, faithfulness, gentleness, self-control" (Gal. 5:22–23 NASB). These emotions are indicators on our spiritual dashboard. Whenever we sense them, we know we are walking in the Spirit. Whenever we lack them, we know we are out of step with the Spirit.

I sensed his corrective pull recently. I ran into a friend at a convenience store. It helps to know that my mind was on the hot political topic of immigration. I was listening to the radio as I was running errands. Every program was loaded with people and their opinions regarding a recently imposed federal ruling on border policy.

All I wanted was coffee and a breakfast taco. The Holy Spirit gave me more than I requested. I was glad to see my friend, shake his hand, and ask about life. He's a cheerful fellow, always quick with a joke or a laugh. Today there was neither. He was solemn. He didn't tell me why, and I didn't ask, but then the Holy Spirit gave me a . . . What was that word? *Push.*

I was already out the door, coffee in one hand, car keys in the other, when I thought about his wife. Somehow I knew she was un-documented. How I knew I could not recall, but I knew. And I knew I needed to talk to him.

I did not want to do so. I had a busy day ahead for one thing. I didn't know what I would say for another. Besides, what if he didn't want to talk? What if the issue was personal? What if I found out something I did not really want to know? I had my reasons, but the Holy Spirit didn't ask my opinion. The prompting was so strong that to disregard it would have been disobedient.

He was still in the store, so I walked back in. "Hey, I, uh, I was just wondering. All this stuff about immigration . . . You guys doing okay?"

Within a moment his eyes watered. He looked around to see if anyone was watching or listening. "Why do you ask?"

"Just curious."

"Actually," he said, "we're in a bit of trouble."

He'd been told to keep his wife indoors lest she be snatched off the streets and taken back to Mexico. He'd been hustled by an immi-gration lawyer. He was low on money, out of options, and increasingly convinced that the world was against him.

It just so happened I had a few ideas. Within a week he had honest counsel, resources to pay the bill, and reason to sleep well at night. All because the Holy Spirit gave me a push.

I do not know exactly how God does this work. The sequence, timetable, and pace are not disclosed to us. What we know is this: "God is working in you to help you want to do and be able to do what pleases him" (Phil. 2:13 NCV). The same hand that pushed the rock from the tomb can shove away your doubt. The same power that stirred the still heart of Christ can stir your flagging faith. The same strength that put Satan on his heels can, and will, defeat Satan in your life.

Make it your aim to sense, see, and hear the Spirit of God. Would you use a two-legged tripod? Two-wheeled trike? Two-sided prism? Of course not. Avail yourself of all God has to offer. Fix your heart on this promise: "You will receive power when the Holy Spirit comes on you" (Acts 1:8).

CHAPTER 13

Justice Will Prevail

GOD'S PROMISE

For he has set a day when he will judge the world.

—Acts 17:31

On December 14, 2012, seven-year-old Daniel Barden awoke early. The dark sky outside their Newtown, Connecticut, home was turning red-orange. Christmas lights illuminated the rooflines of neighboring homes.

"Isn't that beautiful?" he asked his father, who took a picture of the scene. The morning was full of tender moments. At one point Daniel ran down the driveway in pj's and flip-flops to hug and kiss his brother as he left for school. He made a point to hug his sister, Natalie, before she left. He and his dad played "Jingle Bells" on the piano. Later Daniel hurried down the stairs with a toothbrush in his mouth so he wouldn't miss the chance to tell his mother goodbye before she left for work. All in all it was a joy-filled, carefree morning.

No one ever imagined it would be Daniel's last. He was one of twenty children and six adults shot to death by a deranged gunman at Sandy Hook Elementary School later that morning.[1]

Sandy Hook wasn't the first massacre in American history. But it seemed the cruelest. This wasn't a gathering of adults; it was a classroom of kids. This wasn't a war zone; it was a quiet neighborhood. These weren't gangsters; they were backpack-toting, snack pack–eating, Santa Claus–loving, elementary-age children. It was the Christmas season, for crying out loud.

The kids didn't deserve such a death. Their parents don't deserve such grief. And we received an all-too-common reminder: life isn't fair.

When did you learn those words? *It's not fair.* What deed exposed you to the imbalanced scales of life? Did a car wreck leave you fatherless?

Did friends forget you, a teacher ignore you, an adult abuse you? Have you ever prayed the psalmist's prayer: "O Lord, how long will you look on?" (Ps. 35:17 GOD'S WORD). When did you first ask the prophet's question: "Why does the way of the wicked prosper?" (Jer. 12:1). Why indeed? Why do drug peddlers get rich? Sex offenders get off? Charlatans get elected? Murderers get out? Cheaters get by with it? Scoundrels get rewarded? Hypocrites get chosen?

How long will injustice flourish? God's answer is direct: not long. Scripture reveals a somber promise: "For [God] has set a day when he will judge the world" (Acts 17:31).

He is not sitting idly by. He is not twiddling his thumbs. Every flip of the calendar brings us closer to the day in which God will judge all evil. To "set" means to "single out."[2] The Judgment Day has been chosen. The hour is marked and the moment reserved. Judgment is not a possibility but a stark reality.

"Judgment Day" is an unpopular term. We dislike the image of a great hour of reckoning. Which is ironic. We disdain judgment, but we value justice, yet the second is impossible without the first. One can't have justice without judgment. For that reason "we must all appear before the judgment seat of Christ, so that each of us may receive what is due us for the things done while in the body, whether good or bad" (2 Cor. 5:10).

The Greek word for judgment seat is *béma*. The term denotes a court in session, a place where the judge is present and the verdicts are declared. "Pilate was sitting on the judge's [*béma*] seat" (Matt. 27:19).

John's apocalyptic language calls the judgment seat the "great white throne."

> Then I saw a great white throne and him who was seated on it. The
> earth and the heavens fled from his presence, and there was no place

for them. And I saw the dead, great and small, standing before the throne, and books were opened. Another book was opened, which is the book of life. The dead were judged according to what they had done as recorded in the books. (Rev. 20:11–12)

This judgment takes place after the Millennium and after Satan, the beast, and the false prophet are thrown into the lake of fire (Rev. 20:7–10). Books that contain records of everyone's deeds, good or evil, will be opened (v. 12), and God will reward or punish each one accordingly.[3]

Another book, the book of life, reveals each person's eternal destiny. The names of God's redeemed children appear in this book. It was inscribed by God "from the creation of the world" (Rev. 17:8). Anyone whose name is "not found written in the book of life" will be "thrown into the lake of fire" (Rev. 20:15).

While it is clear that the Great White Throne judgment is the final judgment, Christians disagree on who will be judged. Some Christians believe there will be three separate judgments: a judgment of the nations (Matt. 25:31–46); a judgment of believers' works, often referred to as the "judgment seat [béma] of Christ" (2 Cor. 5:10); and the Great White Throne judgment at the end of the Millennium (Rev. 20:11–15), when unbelievers will be judged according to their works and sentenced to everlasting punishment in the lake of fire.

Other students of Scripture see the three judgments as elements of one major judgment. Regardless of the number of judgments, there will be a final, all-consuming rendering. All unbelievers will be judged by Christ. All believers will be judged through Christ. Unbelievers will be punished, and believers will be saved by grace and applauded for their works (Matt. 16:27).

From his throne Jesus will forever balance the scales of fairness. He will do so through three declarations:

1. He will publicly pardon his people.

Paul declared to the Corinthians "we must all appear before the judgment seat of Christ" (2 Cor. 5:10). "We" includes all humanity. Paul didn't exclude his name from this list, nor can we.

We may want to. Especially when we consider that this will be "the day when God judges people's secrets through Jesus Christ" (Rom. 2:16). I don't want you to hear my secret thoughts. I don't want my congregation to know the sermons I dreaded or conversations I avoided. Why will Christ expose every deed and every desire of the Christian heart? For the sake of justice. He must declare each sin forgiven.

God filters his verdict through Jesus. Believers won't stand before the bench alone. Jesus will be at our side. As the sin is disclosed, so is the forgiveness.

> "Max lied to his teacher." Jesus: "I took his punishment."
> "Max stretched the truth." Jesus: "I died for that sin."
> • "Max complained again." Jesus: "I know. I've forgiven him."

On and on the reading will go until every sin of every believer is proclaimed and pardoned. You may be thinking, *This will take a long time.* Indeed it will. Then again, heaven may have a different time frame. If not, we have all the time in the world. God's justice demands a detailed accounting. He will not permit the hint of injustice in his new kingdom. Every citizen will know that every sin has been surfaced and pardoned. Heaven can't be heaven with secrets or buried pasts.

You won't be embarrassed. To the contrary, you will be stunned. Your awe will grow as the list of forgiven sins lengthens. You will feel toward God what my friend felt as the judge declared his innocence. He was indicted on sixty-six counts by the federal government. His trial lasted three agonizing weeks. If found guilty, he would have spent the rest of his life in jail.

I was traveling when the text appeared on my phone. "The jury is back. The verdict is about to be read." I waited for the next text. And waited. And waited. I grew impatient. I texted a lawyer who was assisting on the case. "Why is it taking so long?" He replied, "The judge has to render a verdict on each of the indictments, one by one. The court records demand a permanent record on each accusation."

It took twenty minutes to read the verdict. My friend stood as the judge declared him "not guilty" sixty-six times. The jury heard him. The legal team heard him. The people who packed the courtroom heard him. The accusers heard him. The court reporter heard him. If there happened to be a maintenance crew in the room, they heard him. Lest there be any question of the verdict, the court entered the same words by each indictment.

> Not guilty!
> Not guilty!
> Not guilty!

God promises the same public proclamation of innocence for you and me. We will stand before the Judge as our lives are reviewed. For each transgression God will declare his forgiveness. The devil will hear the verdict. The saints will hear the verdict. The demons will hear the verdict. The angels will hear the verdict.

> Not guilty!
> Not guilty!
> Not guilty!

The result will be a heaven draped in justice. No saint will look upon another with suspicion. No saint will look into his or her past with guilt. All will be disclosed. All will be forgiven. The public display of forgiven sins will prompt eternal gratitude to our Savior. And as he publicly pardons his people . . .

2. He will applaud the service of his servants.

"He will bring to light what is hidden in darkness and will expose the motives of the heart. At that time each will receive their praise from God" (1 Cor. 4:5).

God will walk you through your life day by day, moment by moment, issuing commendation after commendation. "You gave up your seat on the bus. Well done. You greeted the new student in your class. Fine job. You forgave your brother, encouraged your neighbor . . . You stayed awake during Max's message. I'm so proud of you."

"God is not unjust; he will not forget your work and the love you have shown him as you have helped his people and continue to help them" (Heb. 6:10). Our just God will recognize faithful stewardship. If you invest your treasures to honor him on earth, he will give you more gifts in heaven. If you enlist your talents to his honor, he will give you more talents. The same pen that records our impure thoughts makes notes of our pure ones.

And guess who will be waiting for you at the finish line? Jesus Christ. "Well done, good and faithful servant! You have been faithful with a few things; I will put you in charge of many things" (Matt. 25:23).

My friend Dan is an avid runner. We used to log miles together, but then I got older, and he got stronger, and that is a topic for a book on staying healthy. He went on to complete an Ironman Triathlon at Lake Placid, New York. Of all the Ironman events around the world, this one stands out for its community participation. The final mile of the race is run on the track of the high school stadium. The residents of Lake Placid (population twenty-five hundred) pack the bleachers for the singular purpose of cheering on the finishers. They arrive early in the afternoon to celebrate the winner and linger into the night to wait for the stragglers. Many of the runners don't reach the stadium until well after the sun has set.

Dan was one of these. He'd been swimming, biking, and running since eight o'clock that morning. His legs were cramping, and his feet were sore. Everything inside him wanted to quit. But then he heard the roar. Still miles from the stadium, he heard the cheers of the assembled crowd.

He quickened his pace. He could see the stadium lights in the distance. He forgot the aching in his legs and sensed an excitement in his heart. "I'm almost there!"

Within half an hour he reached the parking lot of the stadium. By now the noise was deafening. He straightened his back and took a deep breath and ran through the entrance. Over the public address system he heard: "And from San Antonio, Texas, Dan Smith!"

The place erupted! People he'd never seen were calling his name. Little kids were chanting, "Dan! Dan! Dan!" Gone was the pain. Forgotten was the weariness. He was surrounded by a huge crowd of witnesses.

So are you. Listen carefully, my friend, and you will hear a multitude of God's children urging you on. Noah is among them. So is Mary the mother of Jesus. Your elementary school teacher shouts your name. So does an uncle you never knew. Do you hear the support of the first-century martyrs? What about the Chinese house-church leaders or the eighteenth-century missionaries to Africa? Some of us have a mom and dad, brother or sister . . . even a child in the stands. They are part of the "great cloud of witnesses" (Heb. 12:1).

God records and rewards your goodness. It's only fair that he does.

And since he is a just God, he will declare the pardon of his people, he will applaud the service of his servants, and . . .

3. He will honor the wishes of the wicked.

Some people will stand before God who "didn't treat him like God, refusing to worship him. . . . They traded the glory of God who holds the whole world in his hands for cheap figurines you can buy at any roadside stand" (Rom. 1:21, 23 THE MESSAGE). They spent a lifetime dishonoring the King and hurting his people. They mocked his name and made life miserable for their neighbors.

A just God must honor the wishes of God-rejecters.

Even our judicial system, fragile as it may be, forces no defense on the accused. The defendant is offered an advocate, but if he chooses to stand before the judge alone, the system permits it.

So does God. He offers his Son as an advocate. At the judgment Jesus will stand at the side of every person except those who refuse him. When their deeds are read, heaven's tribunal will hear nothing but silence.

"You denied my presence." Silence.
"You abused my children." Silence.
"You slandered my name." Silence.
"You ignored my Word." Silence.
"You rejected my Son." Silence.

What response can be given? What defense can be offered? God is right. God is just. No one in heaven or hell will accuse the Judge of injustice when he announces, "Depart from me, you who are cursed, into the eternal fire prepared for the devil and his angels" (Matt. 25:41).

Justice will prevail.

This promise may not matter to you. For some people life feels fair and just. If that describes you, count your blessings. There are others, however, who fight a daily battle with anger. They've been robbed; evil people have pilfered days with their loved ones; disease has sapped health from their bodies. They believe that justice must be served.

I'm one of these people. My brother was robbed. Alcoholism heisted the joy out of his life. For two-thirds of his fifty-seven years, he battled the bottle. It cost him his family, finances, and friends. He was not innocent. I get that. He bought the liquor and made the choices. Yet I am convinced that Satan assigned a special goon squad to tempt him. When they found his weakness, they refused to let up. They took him to the mat and pounded the self-control out of him.

I'm ready to see Satan pay for his crimes against my brother. I am looking forward to that moment when I stand next to Dee, our bodies redeemed and souls secure. Together we will see the devil bound and chained and cast into a lake of fire. At that point we will begin to reclaim what the devil took.

For [God] has set a day when he will judge the world. (Acts 17:31)

Let this covenant abate the anger you feel at the hurting world. Devastations have bloodied every generation. Does our globe have one square mile of unstained soil? The Hutu slaughtered eight hundred thousand people, primarily Tutsi. Hitler exterminated six million Jews and a half-million Gypsies. American bombs devastated Hiroshima and Nagasaki. The Japanese tortured American soldiers. Suicide bombs exploded in Baghdad, and a mass murderer devastated Sandy Hook. It's not right, it's not just, it's not fair that evil prospers. When you wonder if the wicked will go unpunished or injustices will go unaddressed, let this promise gratify your desire for justice. God will have the final word. "God is a just judge, and God is angry with the wicked every day" (Ps. 7:11 NKJV).

Till then follow the example of the women of a Dinka village in Sudan. Government-backed soldiers ravaged their settlement, butchering and brutalizing more than a hundred people. Muslim fundamentalists captured the strong, abandoned the weak, burned huts, and razed crops. The horror, however, gave birth to hope. A remnant of survivors, wives and mothers of the murdered and missing, gathered sticks and tied them together in the form of small crosses. Before they buried the bodies and mourned their losses, they pressed the crosses into the ground. Not as memorials to their grief but as declarations of their hope. They were Jesus followers. The crossed sticks expressed their living faith in a loving God who could and will make sense of such a tragedy.[4]

Do the same with your tragedies. Place them in the shadow of the cross and be reminded: God understands injustice. He will right all wrongs and heal all wounds. He has prepared a place where life will be finally and forever . . . just.

CHAPTER 14

Unbreakable Promises, Unshakable Hope

GOD'S PROMISE

We have this hope as an anchor
for the soul, firm and secure.

—Hebrews 6:19

Long after the kids are bathed and put to bed, the single mom stares at the bills and checkbook balance. Too many of the first, not much in the second. She's called on all her friends. She's cashed in all her favors. There aren't enough hours in the day to earn more money. She stares out the window of the small apartment and wonders where to turn.

Then there is the weary man in the ICU standing at the bedside of his only love. He can scarcely remember a day without her. They married so young. He has never known anything as pure as this woman's heart. He leans over her face and strokes her white hair. No response. The doctor has told him to say goodbye. The husband is all out of hope.

And what about the executive who sits behind the big desk in the corner office? His handshake is firm; his voice sounds confident. But don't let his demeanor fool you. If solvency were a jet, his is in a tailspin. His banker wants to meet. His accountant wants to quit. And hope? Hope boarded a train for the coast and hasn't been seen for a week.

You know the feeling. We all do. Even the cup-is-half-full, sanguine souls who use the lyric "the sun will come out tomorrow" as their cell-phone ring. Sometimes we just run out of hope. When we do, where can we turn?

I suggest we turn to this great and precious promise: "We have this hope as an anchor for the soul, firm and secure. It enters the inner sanctuary behind the curtain, where our forerunner, Jesus, has entered on our behalf" (Heb. 6:19–20).

Look at the key terms of the first phrase: *anchor* and *soul*.

You don't need to be told what an anchor is. You've held those iron castings with the pointed edges. Perhaps you've thrown one from a boat into the water and felt the yank as the tool found its lodging place. The anchor has one purpose—to steady the boat. To weather a blast of bad weather, you need a good anchor. You need one like the tattoo on Popeye's forearm—strong and double pointed. You need one that can hook securely to an object that is stronger than the storm. You need a good anchor.

Why? Because you have a valuable vessel. You have a soul. When God breathed into Adam, he gave him more than oxygen; he gave him an eternal being. He gave him a soul.

The presence of a soul separates you from your pet goldfish. Both of you eat. Both of you have eyes and scales—his on his skin, yours on the bathroom floor. Though the two of you are much alike, there is one huge difference—the soul.

Because of your soul, you wonder why you are here. Because of your soul, you wonder where you are going. Because of your soul, you wrestle with right and wrong, you value the lives of others, and you get choked up at the singing of the national anthem and teary eyed at the sight of your baby. Goldfish don't do these things.

Your soul separates you from animals and unites you to God. And your soul needs an anchor. Your soul is fragile. It feels the pain of death and knows the questions of disease. Your liver may suffer from the tumor, but your soul suffers from the questions. Hence, your soul needs an anchor, a hooking point that is sturdier than the storm.

This anchor is set, not on a boat or person or possession. No, this anchor is set in "the inner sanctuary behind the curtain, where our forerunner, Jesus, has entered on our behalf" (vv. 19–20). Our anchor, in other words, is set in the very throne room of God. We might imagine the anchor attached to the throne itself. It will never break free. The rope will never snap. The anchor is set, and the rope is strong. Why? Because it is beyond the reach of the devil and under the care of Christ. Since no one can take your Christ, no one can take your hope.

> Do critics define your identity? No, because God said, "Let us make human beings in our image" (Gen. 1:26 NCV). That includes you.
>
> Can challenges deplete your strength? No, because "we are heirs— heirs of God and co-heirs with Christ" (Rom. 8:17). You have access to the family fortune.
>
> Are you a victim of circumstances? Not in the least. "When a believing person prays, great things happen" (James 5:16 NCV).
>
> Does God have a place for the small people of the world? You bet he does. "God resists the proud, but gives grace to the humble" (1 Peter 5:5 NKJV).
>
> Can anyone understand what it is like to lead your life? Jesus can. "Our high priest is able to understand our weaknesses" (Heb. 4:15 NCV).
>
> Do you feel all alone with your problems? You aren't. Jesus "is at the right hand of God and is also interceding for us" (Rom. 8:34).
>
> Can God ever forgive your failures? He already has. "There is now no condemnation for those who are in Christ Jesus" (Rom. 8:1).
>
> Is the grave a dead end? Just the opposite. "Death has been swallowed up in victory" (1 Cor. 15:54).
>
> Will the sorrow ever end? Sometimes it feels as if it won't. But God has assured us: "Weeping may last through the night, but joy comes with the morning" (Ps. 30:5 NLT).
>
> Will you have the wisdom and energy for the remainder of your life? No, you won't. But the Holy Spirit does. "You will receive power when the Holy Spirit comes on you" (Acts 1:8).

Life isn't fair! But it will be, "For [God] has set a day when he will judge the world" (Acts 17:31).

Death, failure, betrayal, sickness, disappointment—they cannot take your hope, because they cannot take your Jesus.

In his book *The Grand Essentials*, Ben Patterson tells of an S-4 submarine that sank off the coast of Massachusetts. The entire crew was trapped. Every effort was made to rescue the sailors, but every effort failed. Near the end of the ordeal, a deep-sea diver heard tapping on the steel wall of the sunken sub. As he placed his ear against the vessel, he realized he was hearing a sailor tap out this question in Morse code: "Is there any hope?"[1]

Are you asking that question? Are you the single mom who has no resources? The man in the ICU with no strength? The businessman with no answers? Are you asking the question, is there any hope?

Jonathan McComb did.

The McCombs were the picture of the all-American family. Two young, beautiful children. Terrific marriage. Jonathan worked ranches. Laura sold pharmaceuticals. They were God-fearing, happy, busy, and carefree. Then came the storm. Rain was in the forecast. But a once-in-a-century flood? No one saw it coming. The Blanco River rose twenty-eight feet in ninety minutes and roared through the South Texas hill country, taking homes, cars, and bridges with it. Jonathan and his family sought safety on the second floor of the cabin in which they were staying, but safety was nowhere to be found. The house was yanked off its foundation. They found themselves clutching a mattress, riding white water.

Jonathan survived.

No one else did.

When Denalyn and I visited him in the hospital, he could hardly move from the pain. But the broken ribs and hip were nothing compared to the broken heart. Jonathan tried to talk. But he mustered only tears.

A couple of weeks later he found the strength to speak at the funeral for his wife and two children. It seemed the entire city of Corpus Christi, Texas, was present. The church had no empty seats or dry eyes. For well more than half an hour, Jonathan described his wife and children. He spoke of their laughter and joy and how empty his house had become.

Then he said:

People have been asking me how I am doing and how I can stay so strong and positive in a time like this. I have told them that I have been leaning on my family, my friends, and most importantly my faith. . . . After church every Sunday, Laura would always ask, "How do we get more people to come to church and learn about salvation?" Well, Laura, what do you think? They're here.

A particular verse that I have loved over the years has also helped me along. "Trust in the LORD with all your heart and lean not on your own understanding" (Prov. 3:5). I have no explanation for why such a tragic event like the flood takes place and lives are lost, but I know that God is not going to give us anything we can't handle. I know that we are here for a little while, but trust me—if I could have every bone broken in my body to have them back, I would do it, but it is not our call. . . . Yes, I know that this entire tragedy is horrible, and I have been angry, upset, confused, and left to wonder why. I have cried enough tears to fill that river up a hundred times. But I know that I can't stay angry or upset or confused or continue to ask myself why, because I will find out that answer when my time comes and I am reunited with them in heaven. But trust me, that will be the first question I ask.

I took note of the number of times Jonathan used the phrase "I know."

I know that God is not going to give us anything we can't handle.
I know that we are here for a little while . . .
I know that this entire tragedy is horrible.
I know . . . I will [be] reunited with them in heaven.

Jonathan was not naive or dismissive. He didn't react with superficial, shallow belief. He knew the tragedy was horrible. But in the midst of the storm, he found hope, an unshakable hope. He found no easy answers, but he found the Answer. He made the deliberate decision to build his life on God's promises.

Jesus encouraged his followers to "always pray and never lose hope" (Luke 18:1 NCV).

Never lose hope? Never be fainthearted? Never feel overwhelmed? Never get sucked into the sewer of despair? Can you imagine? No day lost to anguish. No decision driven by fear. This is God's will for you and me. He wants us to "abound in hope by the power of the Holy Spirit" (Rom. 15:13 NKJV).

Abound. What an extraordinary verb to use with "hope."

For about half an hour last week, the sky became a waterfall. I had to pull my car off the road. Windshield wipers stood no chance against the downpour. Every square inch of the highway was drenched. Rain *abounded.* God will drench your world with hope.

I once spent a day in Yosemite forest. I could no more number the trees than I could count the stars. Tall ones, small ones. To the right and left. Behind me, before me. Yosemite *abounded* in trees. God will turn your world into a forest of hope.

I remember, as a child, walking through a cotton field near my grandparents' home in West Texas. The farm *abounded* in cotton. I saw no end to it. North, south, east, west: puffy white balls on all sides. God will grant you a summer harvest of hope.

Could you use some abounding hope? Not occasional hope or sporadic hope or thermostatic hope, but abounding hope?

It's yours for the asking. "Grab the promised hope with both hands and never let go. It's an unbreakable spiritual lifeline, reaching past all appearances right to the very presence of God where Jesus, running on ahead of us, has taken up his permanent post as high priest for us" (Heb. 6:18–20 THE MESSAGE).

Ask yourself this key question: Is what I'm hooked to stronger than what I'll go through?

Everyone is anchored to something. A retirement account or a résumé. Some are tethered to a person; others are attached to a position. Yet these are surface objects. Would you anchor your boat to another boat? Heaven forbid. You want something that goes deeper and holds firmer than other floating vessels. But when you anchor to the things of this world, are you not doing the same? Can a retirement account survive a depression? Can good health weather a disease? There is no guarantee.

Salty sailors would urge you to hook on to something hidden and solid. Don't trust the buoy on the water, don't trust the sailors in the next boat, and don't trust the other boat. In fact, don't even trust your own boat. When the storm hits, trust no one but God. The apostle Paul proclaimed it triumphantly: "we have put our hope in the living God" (1 Tim. 4:10).

People of the Promise make daily decisions to secure their anchors in God. In cases like that of Jonathan McComb, the struggle is a life-or-death battle against unspeakable tragedy. In cases like the one I faced yesterday, it is a matter of snatching a day out of the jaws of pessimism.

I'd spent three days staring at a computer screen writing this book. An hour after lunch my brain slipped into neutral, and my eyes began to cross. I knew I needed to take a break. I live ten minutes from a golf course. So within short order I was on the first tee box, golf club in hand, walking down the first fairway, relishing the spring-day warmth.

My phone beeped. I read the text. A coworker informed me of a staffing change at church. *Hmm, wonder why he didn't ask me about the decision.*

I put the phone in my pocket and decided to give him the benefit of the doubt. That attempt at kindness lasted until the second fairway. I felt a snarl welling up inside me.

He should have asked me.

By hole number three I was gripping the driver way too tightly. On the fourth hole I saw an image of my coworker's face on the ball before I whacked it. Number five was a disaster. I envisioned a shouting match with him! By the time I reached the putting green, I'd resigned, fired him, gone on strike, and moved to Mexico.

You might say I'm prone to overreactions. I can tailspin into a valley of negativity within a matter of, well, within a matter of five golf holes. Oh, you should have seen me, dragging my golf clubs with one hand, shaking a fist at the devil with the other. You should have heard me. It's a good thing no other golfers were out on that Wednesday afternoon. I would have earned some angry stares.

On the path between holes five and six, God spoke to me. He asked me about this book. He reminded me of its thesis. And he didn't have to ask the question. I knew it before he said it. *Are you putting it into practice?* I wasn't. I was standing on the problems of life, not the promises of God.

So I reached into the arsenal of promises and pulled one out. First, this one from the story of David and Goliath: "The battle is the LORD's" (1 Sam. 17:47). And then I remembered these words from Isaiah:

> But those who wait on the LORD
> Shall renew their strength;

They shall mount up with wings like eagles,

They shall run and not be weary,

They shall walk and not faint. (40:31 NKJV)

This promise was the very prescription I needed to treat my irritation. I realized, *This battle is God's, not mine. He is in charge, not me. I will wait on God to work.*

I replied to the text and requested a five-minute conversation. By the time I reached the sixth green, my phone rang. I asked, "Were you going to include me in this decision?"

"Of course! No decision has been made! I was just informing you of one option."

That's all it took. I was fine. The anger was gone. The bad news? The devil got my attention. The good news? He didn't have it for long. The promises of God were a fire extinguisher on his flame.

In the first chapter I told you that the promises of this book are some of my favorites. Now that I've shared my list, I urge you to create your own. The best book of promises is the one you and God are going to write together. Search and search until you find covenants that address your needs. Clutch them as the precious pearls they are; hide them in your heart so they can pay dividends long into the future. When the Enemy comes with his lies of doubt and fear, produce the pearl. Satan will be quickly silenced. He has no reply for truth.

They work, friend. The promises of God work. They can walk you through horrific tragedies. They can buoy you in the day-to-day difficulties. They are, indeed, the great and precious promises of God.

Russell Kelso Carter learned this truth. He was a gifted athlete and student. In 1864 at the age of fifteen, during a prayer meeting he surrendered his life to Christ. He became an instructor at the Pennsylvania Military Academy in 1869. He led a diverse and fruitful life that included stints as a minister, medical doctor, and even a song-writer. But it was his understanding of God's promises that makes his story relevant to us.

By age thirty Carter had a critical heart condition and was on the brink of death. "Connie Ruth Christiansen writes: 'He knelt and made a promise that healing or no, his life was finally and forever, conse-crated to the service of the Lord.' Christiansen goes on to say that from that moment on the Scripture took on new life for Carter and he began to lean on the promises that he found in the Bible. He commit-ted himself to believe, whether or not God granted him healing. . . . Carter lived, with a healthy heart, for another 49 years."[2] His decision to trust God in the midst of difficulties gave birth to a hymn that is still sung today.

> *Standing on the promises of Christ my King,*
> *Through eternal ages let His praises ring,*
> *Glory in the highest, I will shout and sing,*
> *Standing on the promises of God.*

> Refrain:
> *Standing, standing,*
> *Standing on the promises of God my Savior;*
> *Standing, standing,*
> *I'm standing on the promises of God.*

My favorite stanza is the second verse:

> *Standing on the promises that cannot fail,*
> *When the howling storms of doubt and fear assail,*
> *By the living Word of God I shall prevail,*
> *Standing on the promises of God.*[3]

Do the same.

Build your life on the promises of God. Since his promises are unbreakable, your hope will be unshakable. The winds will still blow. The rain will still fall. But in the end you will be standing—standing on the promises of God.

QUESTIONS FOR REFLECTION

Prepared by Andrea Lucado

CHAPTER 1

God's Great and Precious Promises

1. Who are the "heroes of the faith" listed in Hebrews 11:7–34? Why are they considered heroes?

2. In this chapter faith is defined as "the deeply held belief that God will keep his promises." Right now in your life is it easy to believe that God will keep his promises? Or is it difficult? Why?

3. Read Matthew 8:5–11. Scripture often describes how people were amazed at Jesus. Multitudes followed him around in awe of how he performed miracles, healed the sick, and cast out demons. But in this story we see that Jesus is the one who is amazed. Why? What does this say about how Jesus values our faith in him?

4. Max cites several passages that describe why we can trust God as a promise maker and promise keeper:

   "He never changes or casts a shifting shadow" (James 1:17 NLT). God's character is consistent and stable.

   "God can be trusted to keep his promise" (Heb. 10:23 NLT). He is trustworthy.

"God is able to do whatever he promises" (Rom. 4:21 NLT). He is able. His power is unlimited.

"It is impossible for God to lie" (Heb. 6:18 NLT). God does not trick or lie; he speaks only the truth.

- Which of these characteristics of God do you need to be reminded of in your current circumstances?
- How does knowing this about God give you hope in his promises?

5. After sharing the story of his shaky left thumb, Max says he had two options: "I could ponder the problem, or I could remember the promise." What problem are you pondering today?

6. Now consider the following promises from God:

"The LORD is with you" (Judg. 6:12).

"And we know that all things work together for good to those who love God, to those who are the called according to His purpose" (Rom. 8:28 NKJV).

"In this world you will have trouble. But take heart! I have overcome the world" (John 16:33).

- Which of these promises could combat the problem you're pondering today?
- Have you ever seen any of these promises play out in your life? What were those circumstances? How could remembering the way God has kept his promises in the past give you hope that he will keep his promises now and in the future?

7. Peter wrote, "[God] has given us his very great and precious promises, so that through them you may participate in the divine nature" (2 Peter 1:4). The Greek word translated as "precious" is *tímios*, which means "of great price, precious, held in honour, esteemed, especially dear."[1] You probably hold dear a lot of things in your life—your family and friends, your job, or your home— but do you consider the promises of God *especially* dear? Do you hold them in honor and esteem, or do you tend to prize earthly possessions and people over God's promises?

8. How do you need to grow as a Person of the Promise?
   • Do you believe in God's promises but need a reminder of how rich they are?
   • Are you feeling jaded by life and questioning whether God will keep his promises?
   • Is this your first time to learn about the promises of God?
   • Identify where you are right now on the spectrum of faith. Where would you like to be after studying *Unshakable Hope* alongside the Scriptures?

CHAPTER 2

Stamped with God's Image

1. Fill in the blank: God made us in his _____ (See Genesis 1:26.)
   What does this imply about humans in comparison to the rest of
   God's creation?

2. What are some godlike attributes we all have?

3. Scripture says, "We . . . are being transformed into his image with
   ever-increasing glory, which comes from the Lord, who is the
   Spirit" (2 Cor. 3:18). If we are already created in God's image,
   what does it mean that we are being *transformed* into his image with
   ever-increasing glory?

4. We often look to people or things rather than to God to define us,
   to give us a sense of identity. In what or whom do you try to find
   your identity?

5. Talking about the love he has for his unborn granddaughter, Max
   makes the comparison that God loves us simply because we bear
   his image. Do you find this easy or hard to believe, and why?

6. Throughout our lives other people try to tell us who we are.

   • Has anyone ever falsely labeled you? If so, how did this affect the way you saw yourself?

   • If not, have you ever falsely labeled someone else? What were the consequences?

7. To combat the labels others have given us, it helps to look at who the Bible says we are. Read the following passages and consider what they say about your own identity. What truths do they point out that contradict false labels you've accepted about yourself?

   "Therefore you are no longer a slave but a son, and if a son, then an heir of God through Christ" (Gal. 4:7 NKJV).

   "For He made Him who knew no sin to be sin for us, that we might become the righteousness of God in Him" (2 Cor. 5:21 NKJV).

   "Therefore I say to you, do not worry about your life, what you will eat or what you will drink; nor about your body, what you will put on. Is not life more than food and the body more than clothing? Look at the birds of the air, for they neither sow nor reap nor gather into barns; yet your heavenly Father feeds them. Are you not of more value than they?" (Matt. 6:25–26 NKJV).

   "Your eyes saw my substance, being yet unformed.
   And in Your book they all were written,
   The days fashioned for me,
   When as yet there were none of them.
   How precious also are Your thoughts to me, O God!
   How great is the sum of them!" (Ps. 139:16–17 NKJV).

8. Because God is the creator of all people, we all bear his image.
   - How does knowing that all people are his image bearers affect the way you see others and interact with them?
   - How could this change the way you interact with even the most difficult people in your life?

9. Think of someone you know who lives out this truth of being an image bearer of God.
   - How does this person reflect God?
   - Using this person as inspiration, how could you live as an image bearer today?

CHAPTER 3

The Devil's Days Are Numbered

1. Thoughts and opinions about Satan and his role in our lives vary greatly, even within the church. As Max pointed out, four out of ten Christians strongly agree that Satan is not a living being but rather a symbol of evil.
   - What are your thoughts on how the devil is portrayed in Scripture?
   - Do you believe he plays a role in our daily lives? If so, how? If not, why not?

2. The Greek word for *devil* is *diabolos*, which means "to split."
   - How does this definition expose the devil's motives?
   - How does it expose the tactics he uses against us?

3. Read Ezekiel 28:12–17. Max relates this passage to the downfall of Satan.
   - According to this passage, what caused Satan's downfall?
   - What does a person's pride have to do with Satan? (See 1 Timothy 3:6.)

4. First Peter 5:8 says Satan is "a roaring lion looking for someone to devour."
   - Why is this a fitting comparison?
   - Have you ever experienced the devil in this way? If so, when and how?

5. John 10:10 says the evil one has come "only to steal and kill and destroy." Think about those three verbs.
   - What in your life has Satan tried to steal?
   - What has he tried to kill?
   - What has he tried to destroy?

6. Read Matthew 4:1–11. In this passage "the tempter" tempted Jesus three times:

   "If You are the Son of God, command that these stones become bread" (v. 3 NKJV).

   "If You are the Son of God, throw Yourself down. For it is written: 'He shall give His angels charge over you,' and, 'In their hands they shall bear you up, lest you dash your foot against a stone'" (v. 6 NKJV).

   "The devil took Him up on an exceedingly high mountain, and showed Him all the kingdoms of the world and their glory. And he said to Him, 'All these things I will give You if You will fall down and worship me'" (vv. 8–9 NKJV).

   - What strategy was the tempter using against Jesus in verse 3?
   - What strategy did he use against Jesus in verse 6?
   - What strategy did he use in verses 8–9?

7. Now read Jesus' response to each of these temptations:

   "It is written, 'Man shall not live by bread alone, but by every word that proceeds from the mouth of God'" (v. 4 NKJV).

   "It is written again, 'You shall not tempt the LORD your God'" (v. 7 NKJV).

   "Away with you, Satan! For it is written, 'You shall worship the LORD your God, and Him only you shall serve'" (v. 10 NKJV).

   • What was Jesus' strategy against Satan?
   • How can this dialogue inform the way you fight against the lies of Satan in your life?

8. Ephesians 6:12–17 details how we can guard ourselves against Satan.
   • What pieces of armor did Paul list in this passage?
   • Think about an area of your life that Satan seems to have a hold on right now. What piece of armor do you need to fight him in this particular area? How could you equip yourself today with the belt of truth, the breastplate of righteousness, the sword of the word of God, or the shield of faith?

9. Just because Satan roams the earth today, it does not mean he always will. Read Romans 16:20.
   • What does this passage say about Satan's fate and his power in our lives?
   • How can these truths give you hope as you face the Enemy today?

10. How did this chapter change or challenge your view of Satan?
    - Did you need to be reminded that he is a real and present threat?
    - Did you need to be reminded that his power over you is finite in comparison to Christ's power in you?
    - Or did you need to remember that Satan is ultimately defeated and his authority will not stand?
    - How can you apply this knowledge to whatever temptation you are facing today?

CHAPTER 4

An Heir of God

1. Have you ever received a significant inheritance? Or have you ever daydreamed about receiving one? How would this gift change your life for the better?

2. Scripture says we are "heirs of God and co-heirs with Christ" (Rom. 8:17). A couple of verses before this one Paul wrote, "You did not receive the spirit of bondage again to fear, but you received the Spirit of adoption by whom we cry out, 'Abba, Father'" (v. 15 NKJV). What does it mean to be adopted by God?

3. In ancient Rome adoption was serious business. If a father did not feel he had a worthy heir, he could handpick someone from the community to adopt and, therefore, to inherit his land and wealth. According to Roman law this adoption brought four significant changes in the adoptee's identity:

   a. He lost all relationship to his old family, and he gained all rights as a member of the new family.
   b. He became an heir to his new father's estate.

c. His former life was completely wiped out. All his legal debts were canceled as if they never existed.

d. In the eyes of the law, the adoptee was literally and absolutely the son of his new father.[2]

• The audience of Paul's letter to the Romans would have understood this, but how does this change your view of being an adopted child of God?

• Have you accepted that you are an adopted child of God, and are you ready to live out your inheritance? Or do you still need to believe that you have been adopted by God?

4. Read 1 Chronicles 29:11–12. What sort of inheritance do we receive from our Father?

5. The story of Joshua leading the Israelites to the promised land of Canaan is a good illustration for how we, as heirs of God, approach our inheritance. God told Joshua, "Now therefore, arise, go over this Jordan, you and all this people, to the land which I am giving to them—the children of Israel. Every place that the sole of your foot will tread upon I have given you" (Josh. 1:2–3 NKJV).

    God tells each of us the same thing: "Arise and receive the inheritance I have promised you." But we don't all believe in this inheritance. If you put yourself in the story of Joshua, where would you be?

    • Are you standing at the edge of the Jordan, questioning whether God really does have a good inheritance for you in the promised land?

    • Are you pursuing your inheritance but not in the promised land? Perhaps you've gotten off course and you're looking for your inheritance elsewhere—at your job, in your relationships, or in your wealth.

- Or are you living in the abundance of the promised land, receiving the inheritance God has for you?
- If you are questioning God's inheritance for you or if you've gotten off the path, looking for your inheritance elsewhere, what do you need to believe about God in order for you to live in the abundance of the promised land?

6. At the end of this chapter, Max tells the touching and tragic story of Hein and Diet, a couple who hid Jews during the Nazi occupation of the Netherlands. How did this couple live out of their God-given inheritance?

7. How could you live out of your God-given inheritance?
   - What do you feel you are lacking today? Peace? Patience? Love? Grace?
   - How can God meet that need and do more than you even asked for?

8. How does living from our inheritance help show those around us the love of Christ? How could not living out of our inheritance hurt our Christian witness to others?

CHAPTER 5

Your Prayers Have Power

1. What role has prayer played in your life over the years—as a child, as an adolescent, as a young adult, and today? Has your prayer life changed, or have your thoughts about prayer changed? If so, how and why?

2. Early in this chapter Max recounts the story of Elijah in 1 Kings. Read 1 Kings 17:1–7 and 18:20–40.
   - How long did the prophets of Baal call on their god for fire (vv. 25–29)?
   - What excuses did Elijah give for Baal's silence (v. 27)?
   - Why did Elijah drench the altar with water (vv. 33–35)?
   - How long did it take God to respond to Elijah's prayer for fire (vv. 36–38)?
   - Why did Elijah want God to perform this sign (vv. 36–37)?

3. Most likely you've never seen God send fire to the earth in response to one of your prayers, but have you ever seen God directly answer one of your prayers in a miraculous way?
   - If so, how did that affect the way you view God?

- How did that affect your prayer life?
- If not, how has a lack of answered prayers affected the way you view God?
- How has it affected your prayer life?

4. James 5:16 says, "When a believing person prays, great things happen" (NCV). Is it easy for you to believe this, or are you skeptical of the power of prayer? Why?

5. God doesn't always answer our prayers on our time line or in the way we want him to answer them. This can cause us to grow skeptical of prayer or feel as if God is distant and doesn't care.
- What prayer have you been praying that God has not answered yet?
- How does this unanswered prayer affect the way you view God?
- Why do you think God hasn't answered this prayer yet?
- How do you reconcile verses like James 5:16 with not-yet-answered prayers?

6. Fill in the blank: Max says that God cares about our prayers because we are God's _____.

7. When you pray, do you see God as your father and yourself as his child? If not, how do you picture him when you speak to him?

8. How does viewing God as your father affect the way you view unanswered prayers? Why does God sometimes say no? Why does he remain silent sometimes?

9. If great things happen when a believing person prays, we should

be praying about every area of our lives. What have you not prayed about that you need to take to God? How could prayer help the situation?

10. This chapter includes a story about a Christian named Dmitri who was imprisoned in Russia during the communist era. He was in prison for seventeen years, yet he still worshipped God, and he still prayed. What would seventeen years of prison do to your faith and your prayer life? How can you find encouragement from Dmitri's story?

11. Read Matthew 18:19. What does this passage say about prayer and community? How often do you pray with others? How could you incorporate communal prayer into your life?

12. Do you know someone who has a rich prayer life? How has his or her example influenced your own approach to prayer? What have you learned from observing a strong prayer warrior?

13. Since you are a Person of the Promise, what kind of prayer life do you hope to have? What steps toward that goal could you start taking today?

CHAPTER 6

Grace for the Humble

1. In your own words define *pride*.

2. Fill in the blank: God resists the proud because the proud resist

   _____

3. Scripture is clear and direct regarding humility and pride.
   Read Psalm 10:4; Proverbs 16:5; Proverbs 26:12; Isaiah 2:12;
   and Isaiah 5:21. These are just a few verses that describe God's
   disdain for pride.
   • Why do you think the Bible so often addresses this topic?
   • Why does God hate pride so much?

4. How are the tragic tales of Bernie Madoff and King
   Nebuchadnezzar similar? How are they different?

5. Recall an instance in your life when you were prideful about
   something. What happened as a result?

6. How does pride hurt our relationship with others? How does
   pride hurt our relationship with God?

---

7. An example of pride is recorded early in Scripture. Read Genesis 3:1–6. How did pride play a role in the first sin of Adam and Eve in the garden?

8. Right after Adam and Eve sinned, Scripture says, "Then the eyes of both of them were opened, and they knew that they were naked; and they sewed fig leaves together and made themselves coverings" (Gen. 3:7 NKJV).
   • Compare this verse to Genesis 2:25.
   • Adam and Even felt shame after they sinned, not before. How might the emotions of pride and shame be connected?

9. Pride often compensates for shame. It's frequently what we go to in order to cover up insecurities or fears. But pride will never free us from those things. Max says that "wonderful freedom is found in the forest of humility." What does he mean by this? Has pride ever felt like a prison to you? If so, how?

10. Read Romans 8:1–2. What do these verses tell us about our shame when we're in Christ? How could believing that Christ's sacrifice took away our sin—and, therefore, our shame—free us to live humble lives instead of prideful ones?

11. In Philippians, Paul said that knowing Christ changed where he put his pride. Read Philippians 3:4–9.
    • Before he knew Christ, what did Paul boast about?
    • Once he knew Christ, what did Paul think about the things he listed in Philippians 3:4–6?
    • How has knowing Christ changed the way you boast and what you boast in? Or *has* it changed the nature of your boasting?

12. At the end of his seven years in the wilderness, Nebuchadnezzar said, "I praised the Most High; I honored and glorified him who lives forever.... Now I, Nebuchadnezzar, praise and exalt and glorify the King of heaven, because everything he does is right and all his ways are just" (Dan. 4:34, 37).
    - Why did it take so long for Nebuchadnezzar to be humbled?
    - Nebuchadnezzar praised God in these verses. How does humility pave the way for worship? And how can pride inhibit or prevent worship?

13. Spend some time thinking about pride and shame in your life.
    - List specific areas of your life where you think you might be in bondage to pride. Why are you holding on to pride? How could you find freedom in humility?
    - Think of some areas of your life where you feel ashamed. Are any of them connected with the areas of pride you listed in the previous question?
    - What do you want freedom from today? How could the love of Christ help usher in that freedom?
    - What would your life look like if you were free from shame and pride? How would that affect your relationships with others and with God?

CHAPTER 7

God Gets You

1. The incarnation is what separates Christianity from all other religions in the world. What is unique about the incarnation? How is Jesus different from the gods other religions worship?

2. John 1:1–18 beautifully tells the story of the incarnation. What words are used for Jesus in these verses? How is he described? Underline all the descriptions, or write them down in a list.

3. The Greek word John used for "Word" is *logos*. *Logos* would have been a familiar term for his contemporary audience. Greek philosophers had long been using it to describe a central figure or divine being that gave meaning and order to the universe.[3] Knowing this, why would John choose this particular word for Jesus?

4. In many ways the incarnation is a mysterious event that's hard for us to comprehend. Now that you've reviewed John 1:1–18, how would you explain the incarnation to someone?

5. Echoing John 1, Paul wrote, "The Son is the image of the invisible God, the firstborn over all creation. For in him all things were created: things in heaven and on earth, visible and invisible, whether thrones or powers or rulers or authorities; all things have been created through him and for him" (Col. 1:15–16). Later in Colossians, Paul said, "For in Christ all the fullness of the Deity lives in bodily form" (2:9).

   • These verses indicate that Jesus was both fully God and fully man. Why did Jesus have to become fully man?
   • Why did he need to remain fully God?

6. Do you think the divinity of Jesus is important to the Christian faith? Why or why not?

7. First John 4:2–3 says, "By this you know the Spirit of God: Every spirit that confesses that Jesus Christ has come in the flesh is of God, and every spirit that does not confess that Jesus Christ has come in the flesh is not of God" (NKJV).

   • How can you know someone has the Spirit of God?
   • How can you know someone doesn't have the Spirit of God?

8. Max wrote, "Had Jesus simply descended to earth in the form of a mighty being, we would respect him but never would draw near to him. . . . Had Jesus been biologically conceived with two earthly parents, we would draw near to him, but would we want to worship him?"

   • Do you tend to view Jesus through his humanity or through his divinity?
   • How does this affect your relationship with him?
   • How might it benefit you to think more about Jesus' other side?

9. Read the following verses: Mark 4:38; Luke 2:52; John 4:6; and John 12:27. How do these verses indicate Jesus' humanity?

10. Think of a difficult circumstance you are facing now. What aspect of Jesus' humanity could help you connect with him in the midst of this trial?

11. Because Jesus became flesh, God understands us more than we might think. Hebrews 4:15–16 says, "We do not have a high priest who is unable to empathize with our weaknesses, but we have one who has been tempted in every way, just as we are—yet he did not sin. Let us then approach God's throne of grace with confidence, so that we may receive mercy and find grace to help us in our time of need."
    • When you approach God in prayer, are you confident that you will receive grace, or do you fear God's response?
    • Since our high priest, Jesus, understands us, how does that affect the way we approach God in prayer?

12. Spend some time before God's throne today. Approach him, knowing that your high priest, Jesus, knows and understands everything you are bringing to the feet of God. Feel comforted in his presence today, because you have a God who gets you.

CHAPTER 8

Christ Is Praying for You

1. What promise gives birth to unshakable hope?

2. What was your initial reaction to the idea that Christ prays for you? Have you ever considered this before?

3. Romans 8:34 says, "Christ Jesus who died—more than that, who was raised to life—is at the right hand of God and is also interceding for us."
   - Max talks about the Greek word we translate as *intercede*. What does it mean?
   - What does it mean for Jesus to intercede for us?
   - That word is used several times in Scripture. Look up Hebrews 7:24–25 and Romans 8:26–27. What do these verses say about *whom* Jesus and the Spirit intercede for, *how* they intercede, and *why* they intercede?

4. Have you ever prayed for someone else? If you have, then you have taken part in intercession. Considering how fervently we can pray for other people, how does this help you understand what it means for Christ to intercede for you?

5. Read Matthew 14:22–32.
   - What happened while the disciples were on the Sea of Galilee?
   - Where was Jesus, and what was he doing?

6. Think of a "storm" you have been in or perhaps are in right now—a difficult time in your life with dark waters and threatening winds. Did you believe Jesus was interceding for you with the Father during this time? If so, how did it affect the way you dealt with that storm? If not, how could it have changed the way you walked through that difficult time?

7. Max brings up a common argument: "If Jesus was praying, why did the storm even happen?" What does he say about this? What do you think about his answer?

8. In John 16:33 Jesus said, "In this world you will have trouble. But take heart! I have overcome the world."
   - What two promises does Jesus make in this verse?
   - How can this help us understand why we go through storms in life?
   - Read John 16:32. In this verse what storm was coming that Jesus referenced?
   - How does it make you feel to know that Jesus also faced storms?
   - How does it affect the way you view the storms in your own life?

9. Go back to Matthew 14:22.
   - Who told the disciples to get into the boat and cross the Sea of Galilee?
   - How does this change the story for you? Does knowing that the journey was Jesus' idea cause you to see the storm and his appearance in the middle of it any differently?

- How could this change the way you see your own storms? How could this give you hope?

10. This chapter includes the story of successful Christian recording artist Chris Tomlin and how Jesus interceded on Chris's behalf when he was going through a storm. Has a storm ever produced something good in your life? Do you think Jesus played a role in that? If so, how?

11. After the disciples saw Jesus walk on water during the storm, what did they do for the first time recorded in Scripture? (See Matthew 14:33.) Why do you think they were moved to worship in this moment?

12. As People of the Promise, we can be certain that Jesus is interceding for us. Spend some time in worship as a response to this truth.

CHAPTER 9

No Condemnation

1. Max talks about the two different ways we tend to respond to our spiritual debt. We either try to do more to earn our way to heaven, or we throw our hands up in defeat, unable to believe in a God who would require so much of us. The legalist and the atheist. Which extreme do you tend toward?

2. In his letters the apostle Paul often addressed this issue of how we deal with our spiritual debt. Why was he especially qualified to write on this topic? (See Acts 9:1–20.)

3. Referencing Psalm 14, Paul said in Romans 3:10–11, "As it is written: 'There is no one righteous, not even one; there is no one who understands; there is no one who seeks God.'"
   • Who is the ultimate standard of righteousness? (See Hebrews 4:14–15.)
   • How does it make you feel to know that a sinless life is the standard?

4. Read Romans 7:22–25. Does Paul's description of being a slave

to God's law and at the same time a slave to his sinful nature resonate with you? How so?

5. Romans 8 is a central chapter in the New Testament because it lays out the security of our salvation in Christ. The chapter opens with this bold statement: "Therefore, there is now no condemnation for those who are in Christ Jesus" (v. 1).

  • How does that statement help resolve the dilemma described in Romans 7:22–25?

  • The language in this statement is absolute. *No* condemnation. Not a little condemnation or less condemnation but *no* condemnation for those who are in Christ Jesus. Does your life reflect that you believe you are free from condemnation? Or do you live with the weight of condemnation?

6. Romans 8:2 explains why Romans 8:1 is possible.

  • What does verse 2 say?

  • What is the law of the Spirit?

  • What is the law of sin and death?

7. Read John 19:28–30. What happened on the cross? How is that act central to this conversation about freedom from the law and freedom from condemnation?

8. Read Mark 15:37–38. What did the tearing of the temple veil symbolize?

9. In Matthew 11 Jesus said, "Come to me, all you who are weary and burdened, and I will give you rest. Take my yoke upon you and learn from me, for I am gentle and humble in heart, and you

will find rest for your souls. For my yoke is easy and my burden is light" (vv. 28–30). This is not a promise most rabbis would make. During Jesus' day there were many rabbis who had groups of followers. A follower of a rabbi was expected to study and learn every law given to the Hebrew people.[4] That was a heavy task.

- Why then was Jesus saying that *his* burden was light and *his* yoke was easy?
- How does believing in Christ bring us rest?
- How could it bring you rest right now?

10. As People of the Promise we can be certain there is no condemnation hanging over our lives. Are you certain of this? If not, what makes you doubt it?

CHAPTER 10

This Temporary Tomb

1. Everyone has a different relationship with the reality of death. Some have come to terms with it and are at peace. Others are afraid of it. Some don't think about it at all. Currently, what is your relationship with death? When you were growing up, how was death addressed? What did people say about it? How was it explained to you?

2. Has someone close to you passed away? What was that experience like? How did it affect your view of death?

3. There are all kinds of beliefs about what happens after we die. Some believe in reincarnation; others believe we disappear into nothingness. But the Christian faith has a unique take on death. Read Luke 23:40–43.
   - What does this conversation teach us about what happens after we die?
   - What is the paradise Jesus referred to?

4. Max says paradise is not the end of our journeys after death. What happens next? (See 1 Thessalonians 4:16.)

5. John 5 talks about our resurrection: "I tell you the truth, the time is coming and is already here when the dead will hear the voice of the Son of God, and those who hear will have life.... Then they will come out of their graves" (vv. 25, 29 NCV).
   - What images do those verses conjure up for you?
   - Now read 1 Corinthians 15:42–44.

6. Max points out that our bodies will be completely whole after they are resurrected. Imagine what that would look like for you. What physical limitations do you have today? What would it be like to live without those limitations?

7. Beyond our bodies being whole, the earth will be whole as well. Revelation 22:3 says, "No longer will there be any curse." Read Genesis 3:16–19.
   - What curses did God put on the earth and on humanity?
   - What would this world look like without any curse?

8. Even though Scripture is clear about what happens to us after we die and how the best is yet to come for all who believe, why do we still fear death? Why do we still try everything we can to avoid it?

9. Second Corinthians 4:18 says, "We set our eyes not on what we see but on what we cannot see. What we see will last only a short time, but what we cannot see will last forever" (NCV).
   - Max talks about the Greek verb Paul uses in "set our eyes." What is that word, and what does it mean?
   - How could you set your eyes on what you cannot see?
   - How could this eternal perspective encourage you regarding whatever you are struggling with right now?

---

10. No matter what season of life you are in, spend a moment thinking about your final days. How do you hope to feel about death once it is close? What needs to change now in your mindset or in your heart to prepare you for that time?

11. The promise in this chapter is that because of Christ, "death has been swallowed up in victory" (1 Cor. 15:54). Consider Jesus' death and resurrection. How can these events give you hope not only for future glory but for today?

CHAPTER 11

Joy Is Soon Coming

1. What is something you feel hopeless about right now, something that truly causes you to despair, something that when you look at it, you see no way out, no possibility for change?

2. This chapter talks about Mary Magdalene, a central character in the Gospels. How did Mary first meet Jesus? (See Luke 8:1–3.)

3. John 19:25 says that Mary Magdalene stood by the cross of Jesus with Jesus' mother and aunt. What does this indicate about Mary's relationship with Jesus?

4. Read John 20:1–11.
   • What is the difference between Mary's reaction to the empty tomb and Simon Peter's and John's reactions?
   • What does this tell us about Mary and how she must have felt in that moment?

5. Consider your answer to the first question. What is your reaction to hopelessness? How do you deal with it?

6. Romans 5:3–5 is one of the most beloved passages in Scripture about hope. Paul wrote, "We also glory in tribulations, knowing that tribulation produces perseverance; and perseverance, character; and character, hope. Now hope does not disappoint, because the love of God has been poured out in our hearts by the Holy Spirit who was given to us" (NKJV).
   - According to these verses, what precedes hope?
   - The Greek word used for *perseverance* in this passage is *hupomoné*. One definition of *hupomoné* is "enduring, patient, steadfast."[5] How could suffering produce patient, steadfast waiting?
   - How did Mary model a *hupomoné* type of perseverance after she saw the empty tomb?

7. Think back on a time you felt hopeless in another area of your life.
   - What happened in that scenario?
   - Do you see any purpose in that suffering?
   - Did it produce any of the fruit—perseverance, character, or hope—Paul talked about in Romans 5:3–5?

8. Psalm 30:5 says, "Weeping may last through the night, but joy comes with the morning" (NLT). Read the rest of the story of Mary at the tomb in John 20:11–18.
   - How does Mary's experience at the tomb reflect this truth that joy comes with the morning?
   - How does this story reflect what we learned about hope in Romans 5:3–5?

9. Mary was certain Jesus was dead because she had watched him die. She was certain his body had been stolen from the grave because she had found his tomb empty. However, her despair

turned to unbelievable hope as soon as Jesus said her name (John 20:16).

- What does this tell you about the circumstance that seems hopeless to you now?
- Could Jesus be saying your name even in the midst of this? When have you heard his voice or seen him work during this difficult time?

10. Max said that the greatest news in the world is not that God made the world. What is the greatest news?
    - How could knowing that God sees you and loves you give you hope?
    - Could you find hope in your seemingly hopeless circumstance even if that circumstance doesn't change?

11. End this time by reading Psalm 103:8–13. Insert yourself into the passage: "GOD is sheer mercy and grace; not easily angered, he's rich in love *for me*. He doesn't endlessly nag and scold *me*, nor hold grudges forever. He doesn't treat *me* as *my* sins deserve, nor pay *me* back in full for *my* wrongs. As high as heaven is over the earth, so strong is his love *for me*. And as far as sunrise is from sunset, he has separated *me* from *my* sins. As parents feel for their children, GOD feels for *me*" (THE MESSAGE).

CHAPTER 12

You Will Have Power

1. What comes to mind when you think about the Holy Spirit?
   What sorts of images or experiences does that stir up?

2. The first time we read about the Holy Spirit is in the creation
   story in Genesis 1:2: "The earth was without form, and void;
   and darkness was on the face of the deep. And the Spirit of God
   was hovering over the face of the waters" (NKJV). What does
   this early mention of the Holy Spirit in the Bible tell us about
   the importance of the Holy Spirit?

3. The Trinity is made up of three parts: Father, Son, and Holy
   Spirit.
   - When you think about your faith, do you see the Father, the
     Son, or the Holy Spirit as playing the central role? Why is this?
   - Which one of the Trinity do you most often pray to, and why?
   - Do you see the Holy Spirit as an active part of your daily life? If
     so, how? If not, why not?

4. What four words does Max use to describe how the Holy Spirit
   interacts with us?

5. Read Ephesians 1:13–21.
   - What does this passage say about the power of the Holy Spirit in us?
   - Ephesians 1:19–20 says the same power that raised Christ from the dead lives in us. What do you think about that? Is that easy or difficult for you to believe, and why?

6. Galatians 5:22–23 lists the fruit of the Holy Spirit as "love, joy, peace, patience, kindness, goodness, faithfulness, gentleness, and self-control" (NLT).
   - How do we bear this type of fruit?
   - What role does the Holy Spirit play in our bearing fruit?

7. Max says, "Saints are never told to create unity but rather to keep the unity the Spirit provides. Harmony is always an option, because the Spirit is always present."
   - What do you think about this statement?
   - What has been your experience with unity among believers?
   - How could the Holy Spirit bring unity to your community?

8. Read John 16:12–15.
   - What does this passage say about the role of the Holy Spirit in discipleship?
   - How does the Holy Spirit guide us in truth?
   - When you look back over your Christian journey, how has the Holy Spirit revealed truth to you?

9. The Holy Spirit gives us power, he creates unity among the saints, he guides us in truth, and he also makes us holy. Another word for *holy* is *sanctified*. First Corinthians 6:11 says, "But you were washed, but you were sanctified, but you were justified

in the name of the Lord Jesus and by the Spirit of our God"
(NKJV).

- The Greek word for *sanctified* means "to separate from profane
  things and dedicate to God."[6] What area of your life has the
  Holy Spirit sanctified?

- Second Corinthians 3:18 says, "But we all, with unveiled
  face, beholding as in a mirror the glory of the Lord, are being
  transformed into the same image from glory to glory, just as by
  the Spirit of the Lord" (NKJV). Our salvation is a one-time event,
  but the process of sanctification, of becoming more holy, is an
  ongoing one. What area of your life has not been sanctified yet?

- Sometimes we try to take the work of sanctification upon
  ourselves. We do as Paul said, "After starting your new lives in
  the Spirit, why are you now trying to become perfect by your
  own human effort?" (Gal. 3:3 NLT). Are there any areas of your
  life in which you are trying to sanctify yourself? How could you
  allow the Holy Spirit back into that process?

10. Are you producing the fruit of the Spirit? Are you loving,
    joyful, peaceful, patient, kind, good, faithful, gentle, and self-
    controlled? Or are you lacking the fruit of the Spirit? Spend
    some time assessing this.
    - Where are you allowing the Holy Spirit to work?
    - Where are you not allowing him to work?

CHAPTER 13

Justice Will Prevail

1. Identify something that happened in your life that wasn't fair. How did this event make you feel? How did this event affect the way you view God?

2. Before reading this chapter what did you know about Judgment Day?
   - If you were raised going to church, did your church often talk about God's judgment? If so, how did you receive this message?
   - If you were not raised hearing about God's judgment, how did you receive the message in this chapter?

3. Read what Scripture says about God's judgment in the following passages: Matthew 12:36; Acts 17:30–31; Romans 14:10; 2 Corinthians 5:10; and Revelation 20:11–12.
   - When will the Judgment Day happen?
   - Who will be judged?
   - How will they be judged?

4. This idea of justice and judgment is a double-edged sword. On one hand it's hopeful to know that God will judge those who

have treated us wrong. On the other hand it's unsettling to know that we also will be judged. How do you feel about this tension?

5. What role will Christ play in our judgment? (See Romans 2:16.)

6. Our complete forgiveness will never be more evident than when we are being judged with Christ beside us. Do you feel fully forgiven by God?
   • If not, what sin or baggage are you still holding on to?
   • What part of your life do you not believe has been forgiven?

7. Max points out that on Judgment Day we will not only be judged for our wrongs, but also our good deeds will be recognized. As Hebrews 6:10 says, "God is not unjust; he will not forget your work and the love you have shown him as you have helped his people and continue to help them."
   • Have you ever done a good deed that went unrecognized? Were you expecting recognition but never received it? What was that experience like? Was it disappointing not to be recognized for your work?
   • Knowing that God sees everything you do, how are you encouraged to do good even if you are never recognized for it?

8. The parable of the talents tells the story of three servants who were entrusted with money from their master. Read the parable in Matthew 25:14–30.
   • What does the talent symbolize in this story?
   • What do the actions of the first two servants, who multiplied their talents, symbolize?
   • What do the actions of the last servant, who buried his talent in the ground, symbolize?

- What did the master mean when he said, "For whoever has will be given more, and they will have an abundance. Whoever does not have, even what they have will be taken from them" (Matt. 25:29)?

9. The master told the first two servants, "Well done, good and faithful servant! You have been faithful with a few things; I will put you in charge of many things. Come and share your master's happiness!" (Matt. 25:21, 23). We all long to hear these words on Judgment Day.
   - What do you hope Jesus will commend you for? What do you hope to have been faithful with?
   - What gifts do you believe God has given you that you could use for kingdom work? How could you be more fruitful with what you have been given?

10. People of the Promise have no reason to fear Judgment Day. And People of the Promise can have faith that God will bring justice to all things.
    - Do you fear God's judgment? Spend some time talking to him about your fears.
    - Is there a circumstance or person in your life that you believe needs justice or God's judgment? Bring that person or circumstance to Christ. Ask him to help you surrender the situation to God's sovereign judgment so you don't have to carry the weight of it anymore.

CHAPTER 14

Unbreakable Promises, Unshakable Hope

1. This chapter talks about hope as an anchor. How is hope an anchor for the soul?

2. Hebrews 6:19–20 says, "We have this hope as an anchor for the soul, firm and secure. It enters the inner sanctuary behind the curtain, where our forerunner, Jesus, has entered on our behalf." The inner sanctuary is the Holy of Holies. Before Christ's death on the cross, only high priests could enter this part of the temple, and they could enter only once a year to offer a sacrifice to God on behalf of the people.
   - What is the significance of Jesus' entering the Holy of Holies on our behalf?
   - What does this have to do with hope? Ultimately what is our hope rooted in?

3. Review the promises given in this book:
   God has given you his very great and precious promises.
   You are stamped with God's image.

The devil's days are numbered.
You are an heir of God.
Your prayers have power.
There is grace for the humble.
God gets you.
Christ is praying for you.
There is no condemnation for those who are in Christ Jesus.
This tomb is temporary.
Joy is soon coming.
You will have power through the Holy Spirit.
Justice will prevail.

- How does Jesus make each of these promises possible? Or how does he fulfill each promise?
- What kind of hope do we have apart from Christ?

4. Fill in the blanks: "Since no one can take your _____, no one can take your _____."

5. Max shares the tragic story of Jonathan McComb, a man who lost his wife and two children in a flood. How did you react to the words Jonathan spoke at his family's funeral?

6. Have you ever felt hope in the midst of tragedy? What did it feel like? Why did you have hope even though the situation appeared hopeless?

7. Think about what your hope is anchored to right now.
   - Is it anchored to the promises of God through Christ, or if you're honest, is it anchored to something else?

- A good way to test this is to ask yourself, "What is something, or someone, I cannot live without?" Whatever or whoever that is, that is where your hope is anchored.
- What keeps us from anchoring our hope in God's promises?

8. Isaiah 40:31 offers a beautiful promise: "But those who *wait* on the LORD shall renew their strength; they shall mount up with wings like eagles, they shall run and not be weary, they shall walk and not faint" (NKJV, emphasis mine). The New International Version translates this verse as "but those who *hope* in the LORD will renew their strength" (emphasis mine). The Hebrew word translated here both as "wait" and "hope" is *qavah*. It means both to wait and to hope.[7] How do we wait on the Lord with hope?

9. Go back and read the list of promises in question 3.
- Which one of these promises do you need the most right now? Why?
- How could you stand on that promise today?

10. This book does not include every promise made by God, because the Bible is full of God's promises. Make a list of other promises God has made that are special to you.

11. You are a Person of the Promise. After reading this book, what does that mean to you?
- How can believing that you are a Person of the Promise change the way you interact with God, with others, and with yourself?
- How can being a Person of the Promise give you unshakable hope?

12. Declare these words over your life: *I will build my life on the promises of God. Since his promises are unbreakable, my hope will be unshakable. The winds will still blow. The rain will still fall. But in the end I will be standing—standing on the promises of God.*

Notes

Chapter 1: God's Great and Precious Promises

1. "Religion: Promises," *Time*, December 24, 1956, http://content.time.com /time/magazine/article/0,9171,808851,00.html.
2. Sally C. Curtin, Margaret Warner, and Holly Hedegaard, "Increase in Suicide in the United States, 1999–2014," *NCHS Data Brief*, no. 241 (Hyattsville, MD: National Center for Health Statistics, 2016). Digital copy at https://www.cdc.gov/nchs/data/databriefs/db241.pdf.
3. Dwight L. Moody, *How to Study the Bible*, updated ed. (Abbotsford, WI: Aneko Press, 2017), 114–15.

Chapter 3: The Devil's Days Are Numbered

1. Jim Burgess, "Spectators Witness History at Manassas," *Hallowed Ground Magazine*, spring 2011, https://www.civilwar.org/learn/articles/spectators -witness-history-manassas.
2. Ibid.
3. Ibid.
4. Ibid.
5. Louis J. Cameli, *The Devil You Don't Know: Recognizing and Resisting Evil in Everyday Life* (Notre Dame, IN: Ave Maria Press, 2011), 79.
6. "Most American Christians Do Not Believe That Satan or the Holy Spirit Exist," Barna, April 13, 2009, https://www.barna.com/research/most -american-christians-do-not-believe-that-satan-or-the-holy-spirit-exist/.

7. Carter Conlon with Leslie Quon, *Fear Not: Living Courageously in Uncertain Times* (Ventura, CA: Regal Books, 2012), 52–53.

Chapter 4: An Heir of God

1. Jeane MacIntosh, "Homeless Heir to Huguette Clark's $19M Fortune Found Dead in Wyoming," *New York Post*, December 31, 2012, http://nypost.com/2012/12/31/homeless-heir-to-huguette-clarks-19m-fortune-found-dead-in-wyoming/.
2. Suzanne Burden, "Meet the Dutch Christians Who Saved Their Jewish Neighbors from the Nazis," *Christianity Today*, November 23, 2015, http://www.christianitytoday.com/ct/2015/december/meet-dutch-christians-saved-their-jewish-neighbors-nazis.html.

Chapter 5: Your Prayers Have Power

1. "Elijah," Behind the Name, https://www.behindthename.com/name/elijah, and "Yahweh," Behind the Name, https://www.behindthename.com/name/yahweh.
2. Nik Ripken with Gregg Lewis, *The Insanity of God: A True Story of Faith Resurrected* (Nashville, TN: B&H Publishing, 2013), 147–58.

Chapter 6: Grace for the Humble

1. Andrew Kirtzman, *Betrayal: The Life and Lies of Bernie Madoff* (New York: Harper, 2010), 232.
2. Ibid., 9.
3. "The Hanging Gardens of Babylon," Herodotus, 450 BC, http://www.plinia.net/wonders/gardens/hg4herodotus.html, and Lee Krystek, "The Hanging Gardens of Babylon," The Museum of Unnatural Mystery, 1998, http://www.unmuseum.org/hangg.htm.
4. Mark Mayberry, "The City of Babylon," *Truth Magazine*, February 17, 2000, http://truthmagazine.com/archives/volume44/V44021708.htm.

Chapter 7: God Gets You

1. Thomas Lake, "The Way It Should Be: The Story of an Athlete's Singular Gesture Continues to Inspire. Careful, Though, It Will Make You Cry," *Sports Illustrated*, June 29, 2009, www.si.com/vault/2009/06/29/105832485/the-way-it-should-be.
2. Ibid.

Chapter 8: Christ Is Praying for You

1. W. E. Vine, *Vine's Complete Expository Dictionary of Old and New Testament Words* (Nashville, TN: Thomas Nelson, 1984), 330.
2. "Chris Tomlin Most Sung Songwriter in the World," The Christian Messenger News Desk, July 3, 2013, www.christianmessenger.in /chris-tomlin-most-sung-songwriter-in-the-world/.
3. Nick Schifrin, "President Obama Writes Fifth Grader's Excuse Note," ABC News, June 3, 2012.
4. Nika Maples, *Twelve Clean Pages: A Memoir* (Fort Worth, TX: Bel Esprit Books, 2011), 129–30.

Chapter 9: No Condemnation

1. M. J. Stephey, "A Brief History of the Times Square Debt Clock," *Time*, October 14, 2008, http://content.time.com/time/business/article /0,8599,1850269,00.htm.
2. Henry Blackaby and Richard Blackaby, *Being Still with God: A 366 Daily Devotional* (Nashville, TN: Thomas Nelson, 2007), 309.
3. Karl Barth, *Church Dogmatics*, vol. 4, part 1, *The Doctrine of Reconciliation*, trans. G. W. Bromiley, eds. G. W. Bromiley and T. F. Torrance. (London: T&T Clark, 2004), 82.

Chapter 11: Joy Is Soon Coming

1. Johnny Dodd, "Amanda Todd: Bullied Teen Made Disturbing Video Before Her Suicide," *People*, October 17, 2012, http://people.com/crime /amanda-todd-bullied-teen-made-disturbing-video-before-her-suicide/, and "Suicide of Amanda Todd," *Wikipedia*, http://en.wikipedia.org/wiki /Suicide_of_Amanda_Todd.
2. Brennan Manning, *Lion and Lamb: The Relentless Tenderness of Jesus* (Grand Rapids, MI: Chosen Books, 1986), 21–22.
3. That is not her real name.
4. Dale Carnegie, *How to Stop Worrying and Start Living*, rev. ed. (New York: Pocket Books, 1984), 196–98.

Chapter 13: Justice Will Prevail

1. Ray Sanchez, "Sandy Hook 4 Years Later: Remembering the Victims," CNN, December 14, 2016, https://www.cnn.com/2016/12/14/us /sandy-hook-anniversary-trnd/.

2. John Blanchard, *Whatever Happened to Hell?* (Wheaton, IL: Crossway Books, 1995), 105.

3. Psalm 62:12; Romans 2:6; Revelation 2:23; 18:6; 22:12.

4. Os Guinness, *Unspeakable: Facing Up to the Challenge of Evil* (San Francisco: Harper SanFrancisco, 2005), 136–37.

Chapter 14: Unbreakable Promises, Unshakable Hope

1. Ben Patterson, *The Grand Essentials* (Waco, TX: Word Books, 1987), 35.

2. Lynda Schultz, "The Story Behind the Song," *Thrive*, www.thrive -magazine.ca/blog/40/.

3. Ibid.

Questions for Reflection

1. Bible Study Tools, s.v. "timios," https://www.biblestudytools.com /lexicons/greek/nas/timios.html.

2. Craig S. Keener, *The IVP Bible Background Commentary: New Testament* (Downers Grove, IL: InterVarsity, 1993), 430.

3. Ibid., 264.

4. Ibid., 77.

5. Bible Study Tools, s.v. "hupomone," https://www.biblestudytools.com /lexicons/greek/nas/hupomone.html.

6. Bible Study Tools, s.v. "hagiazo," https://www.biblestudytools.com /lexicons/greek/nas/hagiazo.html.

7. Bible Study Tools, s.v. "qavah," https://www.biblestudytools.com /lexicons/hebrew/nas/qavah.html.

❧ The Lucado Reader's Guide ❧

Discover . . . Inside every book by Max Lucado, you'll find words of
encouragement and inspiration that will draw you into a deeper experience with
Jesus and treasures for your walk with God. What will you discover?

3:16: The Numbers of Hope
. . . the 26 words that can change
your life.
core scripture: John 3:16

And the Angels Were Silent
. . . what Jesus Christ's final days can
teach you about what matters most.
core scripture: Matthew 20–27

The Applause of Heaven
. . . the secret to a truly satisfying life.
core scripture: The Beatitudes,
Matthew 5:1–10

Before Amen
. . . the power of a simple prayer.
core scripture: Psalm 145:19

Come Thirsty
. . . how to rehydrate your heart
and sink into the wellspring of
God's love.
core scripture: John 7:37–38

Cure for the Common Life
. . . the unique things God designed
you to do with your life.
core scripture: 1 Corinthians 12:7

Facing Your Giants
. . . when God is for you,
no challenge is too great.
core scripture: 1 and 2 Samuel

Fearless
. . . how faith is the antidote to
the fear in your life.
core scripture: John 14:1, 3

A Gentle Thunder
. . . the God who will do whatever it
takes to lead his children back to him.
core scripture: Psalm 81:7

Glory Days
. . . how you fight from victory,
not for it.
core scripture: Joshua 21:43–45

God Came Near
. . . a love so great that it left heaven
to become part of your world.
core scripture: John 1:14

Grace
. . . the incredible gift that saves
and sustains you.
core scripture: Hebrews 12:15

Great Day, Every Day
. . . how living in a purposeful way
will help you trust more, stress less.
core scripture: Psalm 118:24

The Great House of God
. . . a blueprint for peace, joy, and
love found in the Lord's Prayer.
core scripture: The Lord's Prayer,
Matthew 6:9–13

He Chose the Nails
. . . a love so deep that it chose death
on a cross—just to win your heart.
core scripture: 1 Peter 1:18–20

He Still Moves Stones
. . . the God who still does the
impossible—in your life.
core scripture: Matthew 12:20

In the Eye of the Storm
. . . peace in the storms of your life.
core scripture: John 6

In the Grip of Grace
. . . the greatest gift of all—the
grace of God.
core scripture: Romans

It's Not About Me
. . . why focusing on God will make
sense of your life.
core scripture: 2 Corinthians 3:18

Just Like Jesus
. . . a life free from guilt, fear,
and anxiety.
core scripture: Ephesians 4:23–24

A Love Worth Giving
. . . how living loved frees you
to love others.
core scripture: 1 Corinthians 13

Next Door Savior
. . . a God who walked life's
hardest trials—and still walks
with you through yours.
core scripture: Matthew 16:13–16

**No Wonder They Call Him
the Savior**
. . . hope in the unlikeliest place—
upon the cross.
core scripture: Romans 5:15

Outlive Your Life
. . . that a great God created you
to do great things.
core scripture: Acts 1

Six Hours One Friday
. . . forgiveness and healing in
the middle of loss and failure.
core scripture: John 19–20

Traveling Light
. . . the power to release the burdens
you were never meant to carry.
core scripture: Psalm 23

**When God Whispers
Your Name**
. . . the path to hope in knowing that
God knows you, never forgets you, and
cares about the details of your life.
core scripture: John 10:3

When Christ Comes
. . . why the best is yet to come.
core scripture: 1 Corinthians 15:23

You'll Get Through This
. . . hope in the midst of your hard
times and a God who uses the mess
of life for good.
core scripture: Genesis 50:20

Recommended reading if you're struggling with . . .

FEAR AND WORRY

Anxious for Nothing
Before Amen
Come Thirsty
Fearless
For the Tough Times
Next Door Savior
Traveling Light

DISCOURAGEMENT

He Still Moves Stones
Next Door Savior

GRIEF/DEATH OF A LOVED ONE

Next Door Savior
Traveling Light
When Christ Comes
When God Whispers Your Name
You'll Get Through This

GUILT

In the Grip of Grace
Just Like Jesus

LONELINESS

God Came Near

SIN

Before Amen
Facing Your Giants
He Chose the Nails
Six Hours One Friday

WEARINESS

Before Amen
When God Whispers Your Name
You'll Get Through This

Recommended reading if you want to know more about . . .

THE CROSS
And the Angels Were Silent
He Chose the Nails
No Wonder They Call Him the Savior
Six Hours One Friday

GRACE
Before Amen
Grace
He Chose the Nails
In the Grip of Grace

HEAVEN
The Applause of Heaven
When Christ Comes

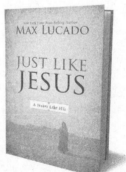

SHARING THE GOSPEL
God Came Near
Grace
No Wonder They Call Him the Savior

Recommended reading if you're looking for more . . .

COMFORT

For the Tough Times
He Chose the Nails
Next Door Savior
Traveling Light
You'll Get Through This

COMPASSION

Outlive Your Life

COURAGE

Facing Your Giants
Fearless

HOPE

3:16: The Numbers of Hope
Before Amen
Facing Your Giants
A Gentle Thunder
God Came Near
Grace

JOY

The Applause of Heaven
Cure for the Common Life
When God Whispers Your Name

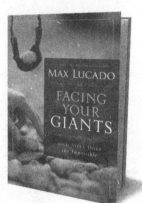

LOVE

Come Thirsty
A Love Worth Giving
No Wonder They Call Him the Savior

PEACE

And the Angels Were Silent
Anxious for Nothing
Before Amen
The Great House of God
In the Eye of the Storm
Traveling Light
You'll Get Through This

SATISFACTION

And the Angels Were Silent
Come Thirsty
Cure for the Common Life
Great Day Every Day

TRUST

A Gentle Thunder
It's Not About Me
Next Door Savior

Max Lucado books make great gifts!
If you're coming up to a special occasion, consider one of these.

FOR ADULTS:

Anxious for Nothing
For the Tough Times
Grace for the Moment
Live Loved
The Lucado Life Lessons Study Bible
Mocha with Max
DaySpring Daybrighteners® and cards

FOR TEENS/GRADUATES:

Let the Journey Begin
You Can Be Everything God Wants You to Be
You Were Made to Make a Difference

FOR KIDS:

I'm Not a Scaredy Cat
Just in Case You Ever Wonder
The Oak Inside the Acorn
You Are Special

FOR PASTORS AND TEACHERS:

God Thinks You're Wonderful
You Changed My Life

AT CHRISTMAS:

Because of Bethlehem
The Crippled Lamb
The Christmas Candle
God Came Near

ALSO AVAILABLE
from MAX LUCADO

UNSHAKABLE HOPE for All Ages!

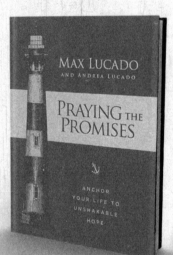

ADULTS

STUDENTS

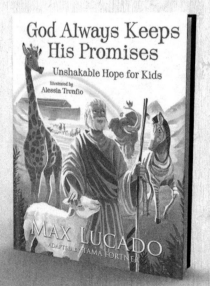

KIDS

Inspired by what you just read?
Connect with Max.